HANDY REFERENCE

Activate Bubble Help with
this icon. Then, whenever
you open a window a
description appears
explaining its function.

Glossary

Assets   Anything of value owned by the business

Bookkeeping   A method of recording business transactions

Creditors   People or businesses to whom money is owed

Debtors   People or businesses that owe money to the business

Liabilities   Values owed by the business

Gross Profit   Sales value less the direct cost of purchased goods

Net Profit   Gross Profit less the cost of overheads

Ledger   The main file or book used to record transactions

Invoice   A notification of goods bought or sold

Trial Balance   A list of totals of all debit and credit balances within the Nominal Ledger

Sales Ledger   A ledger containing customer information

Purchase Ledger   A ledger containing supplier information

Nominal Ledger   A ledger containing accounts other than Sales, Purchase or Cash accounts

ABOUT THE SERIES

In easy steps series is developed for time-sensitive people who want results fast. It is designed for quick, easy and effortless learning.

By using the best authors in the field, and with our experience in writing computer training materials, this series is ideal for today's computer users. It explains the essentials simply, concisely and clearly - without the unnecessary verbal blurb. We strive to ensure that each book is technically superior, effective for easy learning and offers the best value.

Learn the essentials **in easy steps** - accept no substitutes!

Titles in the series include:

Title	Author	ISBN
Windows 95	Harshad Kotecha	1-874029-28-8
Microsoft Office	Stephen Copestake	1-874029-37-7
Internet UK	Andy Holyer	1-874029-31-8
CompuServe UK	John Clare	1-874029-33-4
CorelDRAW	Stephen Copestake	1-874029-32-6
PageMaker	Scott Basham	1-874029-35-0
Quicken UK	John Sumner	1-874029-30-X
Microsoft Works	Stephen Copestake	1-874029-41-5
Word	Scott Basham	1-874029-39-3
Excel	Pamela Roach	1-874029-40-7
Sage Sterling for Windows	Ralf Kirchmayr	1-874029-43-1
Sage Instant Accounting	Ralf Kirchmayr	1-874029-44-X
SmartSuite	Stephen Copestake	1-874029-42-3
HTML	Ralf Kirchmayr	1-874029-46-6
Netscape	Mary Lojkine	1-874029-47-4
PagePlus	Richard Hunt	1-874029-49-0

To order or for details on forthcoming titles ask your bookseller or contact Computer Step on 01926 817999.

SAGE INSTANT ACCOUNTING
in easy steps

Ralf Kirchmayr

COMPUTER STEP

In easy steps is an imprint of Computer Step
5c Southfield Road, Southam
Warwickshire CV33 OJH England
☎01926 817999

First published 1996
Copyright © 1996 by Computer Step

Notice of Liability
Every effort has been made to ensure that this book contains accurate
and current information. However, Computer Step and the author
shall not be liable for any loss or damage suffered by readers as a
result of any information contained herein.

Trademarks
Microsoft® and Windows® are registered trademarks of Microsoft
Corporation. Sage Instant Accounting is a registered trademark of
The Sage Group Plc. All other trademarks are acknowledged as
belonging to their respective companies.

Acknowledgements
Screenshots relating to Sage Instant Accounting are included with
the kind permission of The Sage Group Plc.

For all sales and volume discounts please contact Computer Step on
Tel: 01926 817999.

For export orders and reprint/translation rights write to the address
above or Fax: (+44) 1926 817005.

Printed and bound in England

ISBN 1-874029-44-X

Contents

First Steps

This chapter introduces computer basics and explains how to manage your data input.

Covers

Introduction

Having been involved in training business managers in bookkeeping and accounts for several years I thought it was time to sit down and produce a clear and concise book of how to cope with computerized bookkeeping.

Many people in business may decide to purchase a computer and by running some accounting program think that all their books will be dealt with. However, experience has shown that unless you really know what you're doing, the records often end up in a mess.

Although this book will refer to a popular software application called Sage Instant Accounting, it is also about bookkeeping and accounting principles. There are many books out there explaining the ins and outs of your computer, but there is very little information that will help you in maintaining your business records in an automated system.

REMEMBER

Properly maintained accounts should reduce your accountancy fees.

Unfortunately, many of us are not very keen on "doing the books", but we all understand how important they are in running a prosperous business. So a computer and the right software should help in several ways. It will tell you where your business stands financially and you will be able to make important decisions based on your monthly management reports. This is something that previously you may only have been able to do once a year after receiving the final accounts from your accountant.

I have endeavoured to write in plain English, because bookkeeping does not have to be difficult. I am certain that this book will increase your knowledge and become a valuable asset in maintaining your business.

Introduction to IBM PCs

About 15 years ago the very first personal computers came on the market, invading the cluttered desktops of various businesses. We have come a very long way since the early eighties in the realm of hardware and software development.

Some personal computers have the processing power of mainframe computers a decade ago. Then, only very large corporations had the financial power to invest in office automation, but now that power is available to everybody. Some analysts even go as far as predicting that if a business is not computer literate by the end of this century, they will have great difficulty in conducting their business and may even collapse.

It is the world of data communication and knowledge obtained through the Internet that will prove to be the vehicle on the road to power.

In the last couple of years software applications running your business's finances have also come a long way. The days of working out your "books" on the back of an envelope have gone, and anybody wanting to be in business in the next decade will have to have the basic knowledge needed to produce management reports.

But it will also be necessary to be able to interpret those reports and make sound management decisions based on their result. When using a computer and accounting software, accurate data entry and system management are vital. If your input is rubbish then the output will be rubbish too.

Refer to your vendor's computer manuals for correct assembly of your system. Make sure your monitor and keyboard are connected to the processor. You should have lots of free space on your desk to keep paperwork used for data input.

A printer is absolutely necessary and one thing to consider before you close a purchase is the printed output. Ask yourself if you'll need single or multi-copy output. Some businesses will require multi-copy invoices, credit notes and statements. If that is the case then only a dot-matrix printer will be useful.

Otherwise an ink-jet or laser printer will provide you with better quality output, which can be an advantage when using word-processors that incorporate graphics.

Also a fax modem including the relevant communication software can be a very useful tool, particularly when you want data communication access to other facsimiles or the information super highway, known as the "Internet".

The Operating System

Computers are just big number-crunching machines, and the only thing they understand is a binary code. Binary code is a numbering system using only "0" and "1". For us to be able to communicate and interact with the computer an Operating System has to be designed. One of the most common systems comes from Microsoft, an American software company, and is called MS-DOS (Microsoft Disk Operating System). But today a more advanced system called "Windows" is on the market. Again designed by Microsoft, it uses a graphical interface. Their latest version, a 32-bit Operating System, is called Windows 95.

Sage Instant Accounting runs under Windows. In most cases your computer supplier will have already installed and configured Windows to run on your machine.

Starting Instant Accounting

Switch on your PC and your Windows desktop should be in front of you. The Sage icon should appear in the Program Manager.

Double-click on the Sage icon.

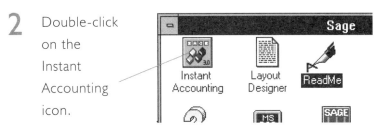

2 Double-click on the Instant Accounting icon.

If you are using Windows 95 (or later) then the starting procedure will look like this:

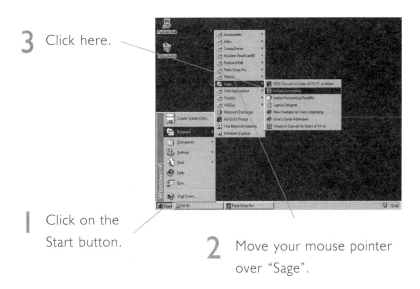

3 Click here.

Click on the Start button.

2 Move your mouse pointer over "Sage".

Instant Accounting Iconbar

The Instant Accounting iconbar offers the following functions, which can also be accessed from the menu bar by clicking on "Options" and then clicking on the required menu item.

HANDY TIP **Move the mouse pointer over the required icon and the description will display itself.**

1 Open the Customer (sales) Ledger.

2 Open the Supplier (purchase) Ledger.

3 Open the Nominal (general) Ledger.

4 Open the Bank, Credit Card and Petty Cash accounts.

5 Open the Product Records.

6 Generate invoices and credit notes.

7 Open the Financials window (i.e., Trial Balance, Profit & Loss).

8 Turn on Bubble Help.

Company Setup

If you are using Instant Accounting for the first time then during the installation process you must enter your company details:

1   Enter your business name here. Use the Tab key or your mouse to move to the line below.

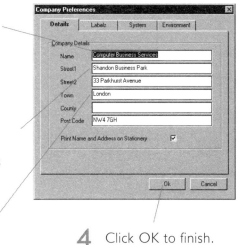

2   There is plenty of room to enter your address as detailed as possible.

3   Town, County and Post Code follow.

4   Click OK to finish.

BEWARE

Ensure that you enter the correct starting month of your fiscal year. You will not be able to enter transactions before that month or after the end of that fiscal year.

Details can be changed when necessary by clicking on "Defaults" in the menu bar and choosing "Company Preferences".

1   Click on Financial Year here.

2   Select the first month of your financial year from this list.

3   Click OK.

Setting Up Tax Codes

Choose Tax Codes after clicking on Defaults on the menu bar to enter or change VAT tax rates. The following codes are automatically set up during installation:

T0 - zero rate transactions

T1 - standard rate transactions

T2 - exempt transactions

T4 - sales to customers in EC

T7 - zero rated purchases from suppliers in EC

T8 - standard rated purchases from suppliers in EC

T9 - transactions not involving VAT

BEWARE

If unsure of the correct EU VAT tax rate then contact Customs & Excise.

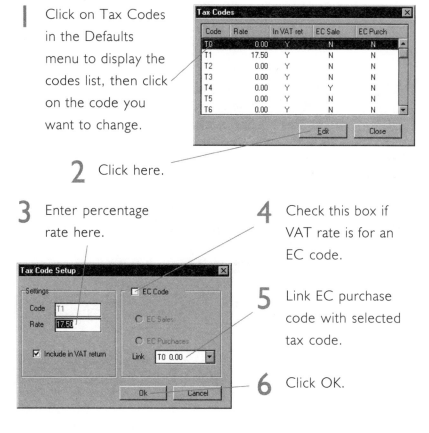

1 Click on Tax Codes in the Defaults menu to display the codes list, then click on the code you want to change.

2 Click here.

3 Enter percentage rate here.

4 Check this box if VAT rate is for an EC code.

5 Link EC purchase code with selected tax code.

6 Click OK.

Code	Rate	In VAT ret	EC Sale	EC Purch
T0	0.00	Y	N	N
T1	17.50	Y	N	N
T2	0.00	Y	N	N
T3	0.00	Y	N	N
T4	0.00	Y	Y	N
T5	0.00	Y	N	N
T6	0.00	Y	N	N

Tax Code Setup

Settings
Code T1
Rate 17.50
☑ Include in VAT return

☑ EC Code
○ EC Sales
○ EC Purchases
Link T0 0.00

14

...contd

Setting Up Customer & Supplier Defaults

In Chapter Four customer records are discussed. Every time you create a new customer, details such as credit limit, etc. are required. First, however, you must enter your Customer Defaults.

HANDY TIP

Default nominal codes (N/C) for customers start at 4000 and for suppliers at 5000.

1. This tab lets you set the defaults which will appear on your customer records

2. Set up Customer Statements and Periods defaults by clicking on the relevant tabs.

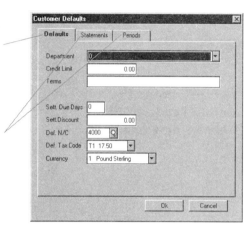

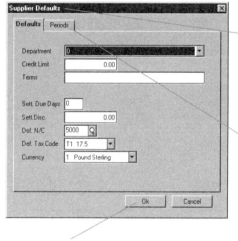

3. Do the same with your Supplier Defaults that will appear in your creditors records.

4. Use this tab to enter your Supplier Periods details.

5. Click OK.

Product, Currency & Control Accounts Defaults

Just as with Customer or Supplier Defaults your product records require defaults too.

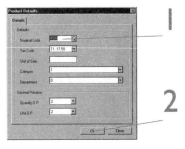

1 Enter the correct nominal account code here.

Use the Finder button to enter the nominal code or to create a new one.

2 Click OK to save the information.

3 Control accounts are used by Instant Accounting to make automatic double-entry postings.

4 There are 99 different currencies to choose from. Click on the one required and then choose Edit.

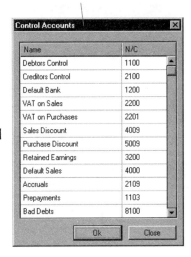

Control Accounts

Name	N/C
Debtors Control	1100
Creditors Control	2100
Default Bank	1200
VAT on Sales	2200
VAT on Purchases	2201
Sales Discount	4009
Purchase Discount	5009
Retained Earnings	3200
Default Sales	4000
Accruals	2109
Prepayments	1103
Bad Debts	8100

You should not have to change the Control Accounts unless you have created your own Chart of Accounts.

Business Transactions

The term *business transaction* is easily defined as a person or persons performing the process of buying or selling goods or services in the view of earning a living or increasing financial gain.

As an example, take a small business like the grocer on the street corner. In the morning you go there to purchase the daily newspaper, some milk and bread and for those goods you hand over some money to pay for them. The shopkeeper accepts the money and puts it into his till. At that moment your first transaction of the day has been performed. But as far as the shopkeeper is concerned there are several other business transactions that will have to be completed before he can close his shop and be assured that there is money left over in the till for the next day.

All the goods that he sold that day were supplied by many of his trade suppliers and all of them agreed to give the shopkeeper 30 days' credit on his account. That way the goods can be marketed and sold before they are actually paid for. So when it comes to the end of the month the shopkeeper sits down and writes a cheque to each of his suppliers to pay for the goods that have been supplied to him that month. Again, by doing that the shopkeeper is performing more business transactions.

When a cheque is written there is no cash being exchanged, unlike when the customer walked into the shop and paid for the goods that he bought. Therefore, from now on we will refer to money as a certain *value* of that *business transaction*.

Entering Password

As prescribed by the Data Protection Act you will be required to enter a password in case you hold detailed information about your customers and suppliers. Once a password has been entered, Instant Accounting will prompt you for it at start-up.

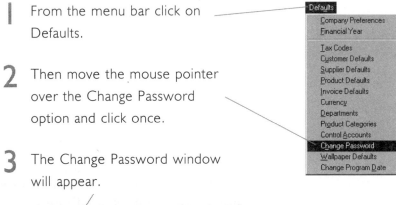

1 From the menu bar click on Defaults.

2 Then move the mouse pointer over the Change Password option and click once.

REMEMBER
The New Password cannot be saved unless it's exactly the same as the Confirm New Password.

3 The Change Password window will appear.

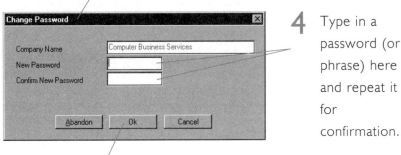

4 Type in a password (or phrase) here and repeat it for confirmation.

5 When satisfied click OK, or Abandon to start again.

As with your credit card PIN number you should not write your password or pass phrase down unless absolutely necessary. You can increase the security by using a pass phrase that includes a "-" or "/" and combining alphanumeric (letters & numbers) characters. This will hinder any intruders attempting to find the correct combination by chance.

CHAPTER TWO

Basic Accounting

This chapter introduces the first steps in bookkeeping, explaining basic accounting principles.

Covers

The Concept of Profit

When many people in business are approached and asked why they are in business, the reply is, "To make money."

Others will have said, "To make a profit," and although some of us could argue that that is the same thing we must realise that they are two very different concepts. The reason for this is quite simple. Every business will "make money", but not every business will make a "profit".

As soon as you walk into the grocer's shop and purchase goods, the shopkeeper has made money. But as mentioned earlier, the shopkeeper will still have to pay for the goods sold, the idea being that he will have sold the goods for more money than he had to pay for them. At the end of the day he has money left over in the till which at that time he considers to be a profit.

But there is, of course, more to profit, which will be discussed later. At this stage, simply consider that you perform business transactions with a view to create a maximised profit over a certain business period.

The Purpose of Bookkeeping & Accounts

Every business needs to keep some sort of record noting every business transaction, in order to create a picture of the current financial situation. Even some private individuals keep some sort of record of their finances so that they know what they can afford.

Properly maintained books will give you an estimation of your sales or liabilities for a certain period in the future.

This is particularly important should you require any financial assistance from your bank. When you ask for a loan or an overdraft to help you over a difficult time, the bank manager will want to see your business records so that he can judge if the business has a good enough cash-flow to be able to carry another liability.

The Inland Revenue will require complete documentation of your business transactions so that your tax liability can be worked out. Then there is Customs & Excise and you will have to prove that you have calculated the correct VAT liability.

For all these bodies to be able to understand your books, the recording of business transactions and the rules of bookkeeping are universal. It is a language that every business manager will understand.

But there is one particularly important reason why you should keep proper books, and that is to be able to produce monthly management reports so that you understand where the business stands financially in the present or future. On such information you then base your management decisions so that you can maximize your profits at the end of the business period.

Gross Profit

As mentioned earlier, you should be in business to maximize your profits. This brings us to the subject of Gross Profit.

Imagine that you purchase an old chair at an auction with the intention of renovating it and selling it on to a friend. The purchase price of the chair is £50; you put it into your car and on the way home you stop at a hardware store to buy the necessary items you'll need to renovate it, at a cost of £20.

At the weekend you see your friend and show him the finished piece; he agrees to buy the chair from you for £90.

This is how you would record your transactions to calculate your profit:

Sale	£90
Purchase (or Cost Of Sale)	£50
Gross Profit	£40

As you can see, Gross Profit is calculated by subtracting your purchase price from your sales price. That is a good way to see the difference between your overall turnover and your Cost of Sale. But there were other transactions and they will also have to be included, as described in the "Net Profit" section on the following page.

N.B. Some business managers mistake their business as their own and sometimes perform certain private transactions using their business accounts. Proper bookkeeping can take care of those transactions and account for them correctly, but a lot of them can be avoided if you treat yourself, the individual, and the business as separate entities. This is called "The Entity Theory".

Net Profit

You should record your Gross Profit and then include the cost of materials purchased, as follows:

Sale	£90
Purchase	£50
Gross Profit	£40
Less Expenses	£20
Net Profit	£20

Once the chair is sold you should have £20 left in your pocket. But what would have happened if the materials needed to renovate the chair cost £60?

Sale	£90
Purchase	£50
Gross Profit	£40
Less Expenses	£60
Net Loss	(£20)

This time you have a "Net Loss". As explained before, you actually have "made money", but your overheads were larger then expected. Hence you have failed to create a "Net Profit". Note, a negative figure is placed between brackets; the minus sign, "-", is not used.

There are a number of solutions to this problem. You could have tried to pay less for the chair in the first place, or the sale price could have been higher to compensate for the cost of the expenses. Business managers have to make these kind of decisions on a regular basis and therefore it is important to maintain your books. A computerized system will perform many transactions automatically to produce the necessary management reports.

The Equation

Let us return to your renovating business. You plan to do this sort of work professionally, and since you have some extra cash you go out and look for a workshop. You decide to put £5,000 towards your business venture and the next day you go back to the auction to purchase your first lot of stock. The furniture items are a resource of the business that are referred to as "Assets". But the money you used to purchase your stock came from your own pocket, and this resource is referred to as "Capital". This brings us to the first accounting equation:

Assets = Capital

There is an ideal shop including a work area that you find, but the rent and fittings are more than you are able to afford. So you decide to see your bank manager, present him with your business plan and ask him for a loan of £5,000. The loan gets approved and now the business owes money to the bank. This is referred to as "Liability", and the second equation looks like this:

Assets = Capital + Liabilities

If the variables in this equation are replaced by the example figures given above, the result is as follows:

£10,000 = £5,000 + £5,000

The £5,000 loan from the bank is used to rent and fit out the shop, which then becomes an asset of the business. Now there are two different types of assets within the business.

First you purchased second-hand furniture that you will restore and use as your stock. Because you intend to sell this stock and purchase more within your first 12-month accounting period, this stock is referred to as "Current Assets".

On the other hand, your shop fittings and equipment (such as the till and furniture) you intend to have for longer than 12 months and are not intended for resale. We call these "Fixed Assets". Now your equation will look like this:

Fixed Assets + Current Assets = Capital + Liabilities

It is similar with Liabilities. Your bank loan will be repaid over three years – this is called a "Long-term Liability". Your rent, however, will have to be paid on a quarterly basis. Because it is a liability that falls within a 12-month period it is referred to as a "Short-term Liability" or "Current Liability". The final equation is:

Fixed Assets + Current Assets = Capital + Long Term Liabilities + Short Term Liabilities

This equation can also be expressed as:

(Fixed + Current Assets) - (Long + Short Term Liabilities) = Capital

The Balance Sheet

In the previous section we discussed the accounting equation and mentioned a newly-formed furniture restoration business. Using the figures from before, the initial layout of your balance sheet will look something like this:

Fixed Assets

Furniture & Fixtures	1000.00		
Office Equipment	500.00		
		1500.00	

Current Assets

Stock	5000.00		
Bank Account	3500.00		
		8500.00	
			10000.00

Less Liabilities

Bank Loan	5000.00		
		5000.00	
			5000.00

Capital		5000.00	
			5000.00

As you can see, the top-to-bottom layout was used, incorporating the last equation:

(Fixed + Current Assets) - (Long + Short Term Liabilities) = Capital

The balance sheet will show the financial position of your business at a certain time. Knowing your separate assets and liabilities, you can record a more detailed balance sheet. Having your reports as detailed as possible will help you to pinpoint any particular problem.

...contd

This time you can include a proper heading such as the name of the business and the date the report was produced. This way, when looking back you can formulate a picture of the business's financial history.

ACME Furniture Restoration
Balance Sheet
11/11/95

Fixed Assets			
Furniture & Fixtures	1000.00		
Office Equipment	500.00		
		1500.00	
Current Assets			
Stock	5000.00		
Bank Account	3500.00		
		8500.00	
			10000.00
Less Liabilities			
Bank Loan	5000.00		
		5000.00	
			5000.00
Capital		5000.00	
			5000.00

Now we come to discuss a new asset account called "Trade Debtors". Many businesses will sell goods on credit, allowing 30 or more days for payment. On such occasions the business will issue an invoice informing their customer of the amount and terms of trading. For example, let us say you restored a beautiful mahogany chest of drawers and sold it on credit. Your customer becomes your debtor and your balance sheet will look as follows:

ACME Furniture Restoration
Balance Sheet
11/11/95

Fixed Assets

Furniture & Fixtures	1000.00		
Office Equipment	500.00		
		1500.00	

Current Assets

Trade Debtors	90.00		
Stock	4910.00		
Bank Account	4000.00		
		9000.00	
			10500.00

Less Liabilities

Trade Creditors	500.00		
Bank Loan	5000.00		
		5500.00	
			5500.00

Capital		5000.00	
			5000.00

It works in reverse if you purchase goods on credit from another business. That way you become your supplier's debtor and at the same time he will be your "Trade Creditor".

CHAPTER THREE

The Nominal Ledger

This chapter will explain the basic principles of double-entry bookkeeping. It starts with debit and credit accounts such as assets and liabilities.

Covers

The Nominal Iconbar

The Nominal iconbar provides features such as account record maintenance, journal double-entries and analysis based on graphs and/or reports.

1 Open the Nominal Records.

2 Open the Nominal Activity.

3 Enter Nominal Ledger journal double-entries.

 Move the mouse pointer over the required icon and the description will display itself.

4 Open the Nominal Chart of Accounts.

5 Open the Nominal Reports.

The Nominal Ledger

The Nominal Ledger, also known as the General Ledger, is very different to the Sales and Purchase Ledgers. The Sales Ledger will inform you of any details relating to your sales, and the Purchase Ledger to purchases made from your suppliers.

The individual sales and purchases are then pooled into certain sales and purchase Nominal accounts. The management reporting programs will extract and use figures from those accounts to tell you how your business is performing at any given time. More about that in the "Financials" chapter.

1 Click on the Nominal icon to open the Nominal Ledger.

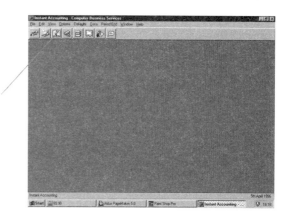

2 The Nominal Ledger opens and displays all existing Nominal accounts.

REMEMBER **The Accounts List in the Nominal Ledger is equal to the Chart of Accounts.**

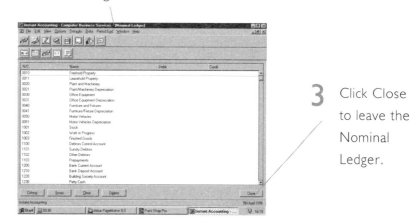

3 Click Close to leave the Nominal Ledger.

The Double-Entry Principle

In the previous chapter the balance sheet and basic bookkeeping were discussed. It would be very tedious if you had to redraft the balance sheet after every transaction. As the word "bookkeeping" implies, your transactions are recorded in a book of some kind, and double-entry bookkeeping means that there is a double entry for each transaction in your book.

The main book in which you make your entries is called a "ledger". Those ledgers used to be thick books or loose leaves in a binder, but today they exist in the form of computerised data files.

Anyone who has seen the double-entry format in a ledger before may have noted that there are two sides to it. You may also have noted in the previous chapter that "Assets" was always written on the left and "Liabilities" on the right of the formula. The reason for that is that assets are always recorded on the left and are called "Debit" entries, and liabilities – on the right – are called "Credit" entries. Do not confuse the term "Credit" here with the way it is normally understood; we will discuss this later when we come to the Bank account. For the time being, simply remember that debit entries are always made on the left side, and credit entries on the right side of the page.

Double-Entry in Practice

Here is the basic rule of double-entry bookkeeping, which you should always keep in mind:

DEBIT the account RECEIVING the value

CREDIT the account GIVING the value

"What is this giving and receiving of value?" you ask. Let us take liabilities to begin with. Remember your restoration business? Before you opened your shop you went to see the bank manager and asked him for a loan. You were lucky, and the bank was GIVING you an amount to the value of £5,000.

You accepted the money and with it you purchased a number of assets for the business, such as furniture and fittings and a till for the shop. So the business was RECEIVING the same value that was given by the bank.

Your first entry in the ledger could have looked like this:

	DR	CR
Assets	5000.00	
Liabilities		5000.00

But you should record your transaction in more detail:

	DR	CR
Furniture & Fittings	900.00	
Office Equipment	100.00	
Current Assets		
Bank Account	4000.00	
Liabilities		
Bank Loan		5000.00
	5000.00	5000.00

For the time being you purchased £900 worth of furniture & fittings, and the till was £100. The rest you deposited in your bank account. ("Why is the bank account a debit entry?" you may ask. That will be covered later. For the time being, stick to the rule that an asset is always a debit entry.)

Let us now apply this to Instant Accounting. You can now make the first necessary entries for your restoration business, using what has been learned so far.

The debits and credits that you have just recorded can now be used to post your first entries in Instant Accounting. Once you click on the Nominal icon the screen on the following page should be displayed.

The Journal Double-Entry

Here is how you would enter a journal entry for an incorrect sale of £100 posted to the wrong account.

1 Enter a reference here. This entry is optional.

2 Enter the transaction date here.

3 Enter the nominal account number (N/C) of the first account here.

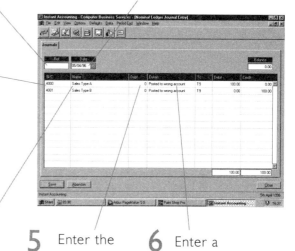

HANDY TIP

The tax code (Tc) will always be T9, unless the transaction involves the Sales or Purchase Tax Control Account. Then it must be changed to T1. If not, the VAT Return program will not recognize it.

4 The account name is displayed automatically.

5 Enter the department number.

6 Enter a description.

7 The tax code will default to T9.

8 Enter either a debit or credit entry.

10 Click Save to post.

9 Enter the double entry on the second line.

Assets

In Chapter Ten the need to enter the opening balances of your Asset and Liability accounts will be discussed, using the practice company, ACME Furniture Restorations. In Chapter Two it was said that accounts like Furniture & Fixtures and Office Equipment are called "Fixed Asset" accounts, due to the nature of their value to the business.

Here are some Fixed Asset accounts:

1. Property
2. Plant & Machinery
3. Motor Vehicles
4. Computer Equipment
5. Furniture & Fixtures
6. Office Equipment

Fixed Asset accounts hold their value for a period longer than twelve months and are not intended for resale. The value of Current Assets, however, will change within your twelve-month accounting period.

The following are Current Asset accounts:

1. Trade Debtors
2. Current Bank account
3. Stock
4. Petty Cash
5. Prepayments

When the balance sheet was discussed it was said that Asset accounts are recorded on the left side of the record and they are referred to as "Debit" entries.

In accordance with the rule that accounts receiving a certain value will be debited, Asset accounts will have to be recorded on the left side.

Liabilities

It was noted previously that Liability accounts are recorded on the right side of your file and are called "Credit" entries. They are called Liability accounts because they are the giver of a certain value to one or several Asset or Expense accounts, representing a value which has to be returned within a given period.

Here are some typical Long-term Liability accounts:

1. Bank Loan
2. Hire Purchase Agreement

These accounts will hold a certain value for a period longer than twelve months, as opposed to the Short-term Liability accounts:

1. Bank account (in case of an overdraft)
2. Trade Creditors
3. PAYE
4. National Insurance
5. VAT
6. Accruals

The PAYE and National Insurance accounts will be discussed in Chapter Twelve.

The Nominal Records

Why maintain a general ledger? When many people in business are approached and asked why they are in business, the reply is, "To make money."

Others will have said, "To make a profit," and although some of us could argue that that is the same thing we must realise that they are two very different concepts. The reason for this is quite simple. Every business will "make money", but not every business will make a "profit".

As soon as you walk into the grocer's shop and purchase goods, the shopkeeper has made money. But as mentioned earlier, the shopkeeper will still have to pay for the goods sold, the idea being that he will have sold the goods for more money than he had to pay for them. At the end of the day he has money left over in the till which at that time he considers to be a profit.

But there is, of course, more to profit, which will be discussed later, in the "Financials" chapter. At this stage, simply consider that you perform business transactions with a view to create a maximised profit over a certain business period.

Let us start with the individual records. When you installed Instant Accounting you may have chosen to use the default Chart of Accounts or you may have created your own.

Using the scroll bar, move down the list of accounts and then select the Sales Type A account by clicking on it.

...contd

2 Once you click on the account it will be highlighted in blue.

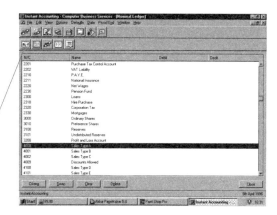

3 Click on the Record icon.

It is best to change the Sales account name to suit your needs.

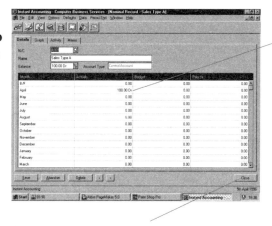

4 In the corresponding month can be seen the transaction and a total below.

5 Click Close to finish.

You can change the budgets at any time using the Global Changes feature from the Data menu.

The first part of this window will only display the total value of transactions for each month with a cumulative total at the bottom. To the right of each monthly total a budget value can be entered, which will be used to create budget and ratio reports.

At the top you will notice that this account is a Control account. That is because it is linked with the Customer (sales) Ledger.

The Records Analysis

The other parts of the Nominal Record window can be very useful to analyse a particular account.

1 Click on the Graphs tab.

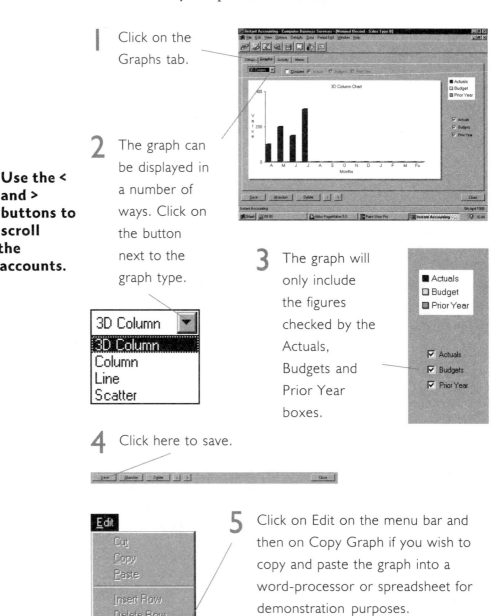

2 The graph can be displayed in a number of ways. Click on the button next to the graph type.

HANDY TIP

Use the < and > buttons to scroll through the selected accounts.

3 The graph will only include the figures checked by the Actuals, Budgets and Prior Year boxes.

4 Click here to save.

5 Click on Edit on the menu bar and then on Copy Graph if you wish to copy and paste the graph into a word-processor or spreadsheet for demonstration purposes.

...contd

The Activity Tab in the Record Analysis
This tab will show the transaction history of a chosen account.

1 Select a range if required.

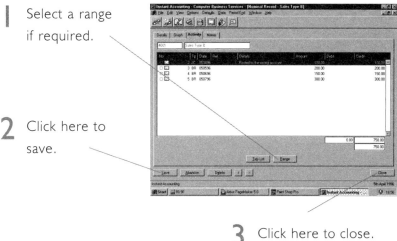

2 Click here to save.

3 Click here to close.

The Memo Tab in the Record Analysis
This tab will allow you to write memos in case there are special requirements for the maintenance of an account.

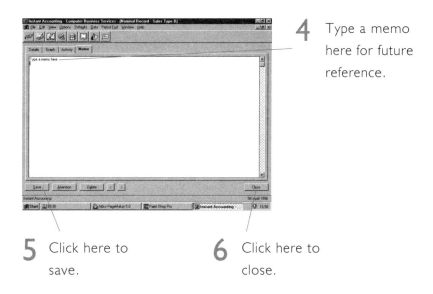

4 Type a memo here for future reference.

5 Click here to save.

6 Click here to close.

Prepayments

Sometimes revenue income and expenses may not have been received or paid for within the set accounting period when the reports are prepared. In case of sales to Customer accounts and purchases relating to Supplier accounts the Debtors and Creditors Control accounts will inform you of any outstanding debts or payments owed.

But what happens when, for example, you have made a payment, such as rent, that will also fall into the next accounting period as an expense? Let us say that you produce monthly management reports and that your rent payments are made quarterly at £900. That clearly shows that your monthly rental liability is £300, but you have paid the total amount in the first month.

If you make a bank payment of £900 in the first month, the Profit & Loss statement will show it accordingly, and in the other two months it will account for no rental expense at all. Therefore, the Current Asset account called "Prepayments" is used. Before the Month End procedure is run, the correct monthly amount is posted to the Rental expense account, making a journal entry. Every month the Rental account should be debited by £300 and the Prepayments account credited by the same amount. All that is left to do is to post a bank payment to the Prepayments account for the full amount.

HANDY TIP

Use the Finder button to choose the Nominal account.

1 Click on the Journal icon.

2 Choose the correct expense account.

3 Enter a description.

4 Enter the amount and then enter the double entry.

Accruals

Something similar to a prepayment occurs when an expense for the current period is not paid until the next accounting period. This time you use the Liability account called "Accruals". It works the same way as Prepayments, only in reverse.

For example, let us say that the electricity bill was paid in one accounting period, but the charges fell into the previous period. The transaction is made using the Accrual and Electricity accounts when the charge actually fell due. When payment was made, the bank transaction was applied to the Accrual account, rather then to the Electricity account.

1   Click on the Journal icon.

2   The Journal window will appear.

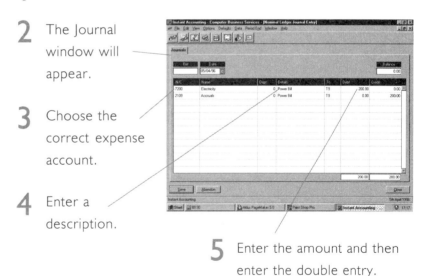

3   Choose the correct expense account.

4   Enter a description.

5   Enter the amount and then enter the double entry.

This accrual should be applied before the Month End procedure is run.

The Chart of Accounts

Instant Accounting has already created a default Chart of Accounts when installing the program, suitable for the following financial reports:

- The Profit & Loss Report

- The Balance Sheet Report

- The Budget Report

- The Prior Year Report

These reports will be discussed in the chapter "Financials".

 | Click on the Chart of Accounts icon.

2 The Chart of Accounts defaults window will appear.

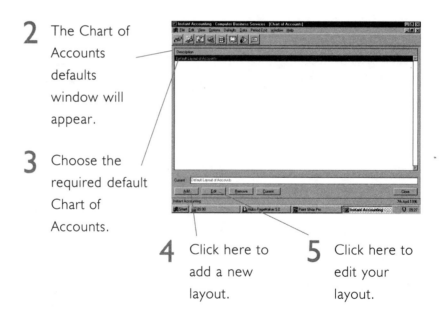

3 Choose the required default Chart of Accounts.

4 Click here to add a new layout.

5 Click here to edit your layout.

...contd

The Chart of Accounts Dialog Box

1   Click on the required category.

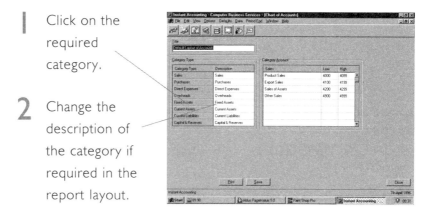

2   Change the description of the category if required in the report layout.

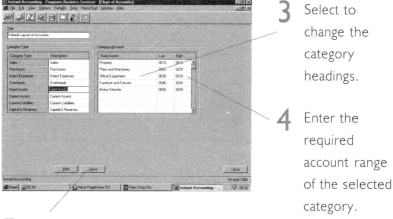

3   Select to change the category headings.

4   Enter the required account range of the selected category.

5   Save when finished.

Each category can be laid out as detailed as possible, choosing selected account ranges. This will be beneficial when you're looking at the financial reports generated to help you make management decisions.

Printing Your Chart of Accounts

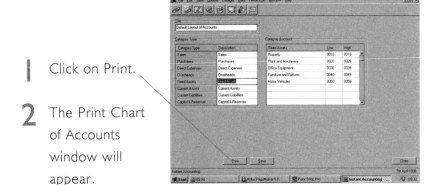

HANDY TIP **Print if you have created your own Chart of Accounts in case you have missed something.**

1   Click on Print.

2   The Print Chart of Accounts window will appear.

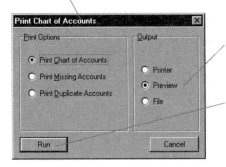

3   Select the type of output required.

4   Click on Run.

REMEMBER **The current default layout cannot be deleted.**

Deleting a Chart of Accounts Layout

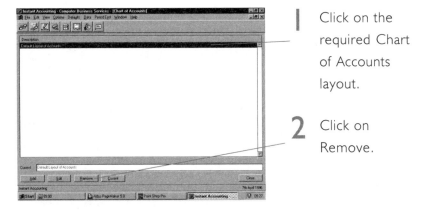

1   Click on the required Chart of Accounts layout.

2   Click on Remove.

CHAPTER FOUR

The Customer Ledger

This chapter explains how to maintain your Customer Ledger, how to create new customer records or maintain existing ones, and how to run a detailed analysis using graphs and reports.

Covers

The Customer Iconbar

The Customer Iconbar provides features such as invoicing, credit notes and reporting.

1   Open the Customer Records.

2   Open the Customer Activity.

3   Open the Customer Aged Balances.

4   Open the Customer Batch Invoices input.

5   Open the Customer Credit Note input.

6   Open the Customer Mailing Labels.

7   Open the Customer Letters.

8   Open the Customer Statements.

9   Open the Customer Reports.

HANDY TIP

Move the mouse pointer over the required icon and the description will display itself.

The Customer Record List

The first icon option on the desktop is the Customer (sales) Ledger. Within this ledger you can perform the following actions:

• Maintain customer records and their details.

• Record invoices and credit notes that you have sent to your customers.

• Print customer statements.

• Analyse your customers' transaction history through reports, graphs and tables.

• Generate customer letters and mailing labels.

Once a transaction has been posted in your Customer Record, it can no longer be deleted.

1 Click on the Customers icon, and the Customers desktop will appear.

2 The first icon on the left is the Customer Record icon.

Be as detailed as possible with your Customer Record input.

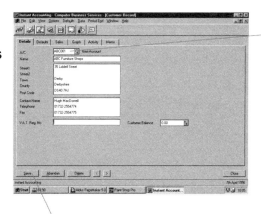

3 The Customer Record window appears and you must enter details to create a new customer, starting with the Account Code (A/C).

4 Click on Save to make the information permanent.

The Customer Batch Invoices

As mentioned in Chapter Seven, "Generating Invoices", the Batch Invoices window is used to input a number of sales transactions for which invoices have been raised.

I   First move the mouse pointer over the Batch Invoices icon and click once with the left button.

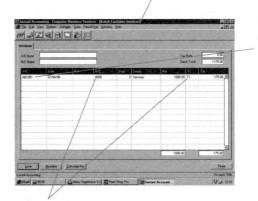

2   The Batch Customer Invoices window appears.

3   Type in the Customer Account Code (A/C) or click on the Display icon just to the right of it to open the Customer List window.

4   Note the nominal account (N/C) default, enter a description and amount. The tax code (Tc) is automatically set at T1 (calculating VAT at 17.5%). In the case of no VAT change this code to T9.

5   Click on Save, and the invoice is posted. After closing the window the Customer List will display the customer's latest balance.

The Customer Activity

The Customer Activity window will display the individual debit and credit entries made within a chosen customer account. Every debit entry refers to an invoice raised, and every credit entry refers to an invoice paid.

1 From the Customer List click on the account whose activity you want to look at.

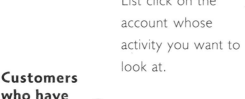

HANDY TIP

Customers who have reached their credit limit are displayed in red.

2 Then click on the Activity icon.

3 The next window will ask you to enter ranges for transaction numbers and/or dates.

4 Click OK.

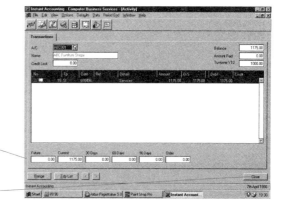

HANDY TIP

To the far right of the Activity window, figures such as Balance, Paid and Turnover YTD (Year-to Date), can be useful information.

5 The Customer Activity window will be displayed. Note the credit period and the aged balance.

6 Click Close to finish.

The Customer Aged Balance

In the Customer Activity section, aged balances were mentioned. These refer to the time elapsed between goods being sold and the outstanding debt of your customer. The average period of credit given by most businesses is 30 days, but they can be negotiated to longer periods such as 60 or more days. Some businesses even charge interest on outstanding invoices.

1 From the Customer List window click on the customer for whom you want to request an aged balance.

2 Click on the Aged Balances icon.

3 The next window will request a date range for the required aged balances.

4 Click OK.

5 This window will inform you of your customers' aged balances due.

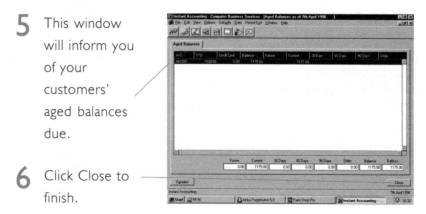

6 Click Close to finish.

The Customer Credit Note

Sometimes when supplying goods to your customers, the goods could be faulty and returned to you, or the number of items dispatched could be less than ordered.

Instead of settling the difference by making the payment due to the correct amount, you may issue a credit note to your customer. This may be a piece of paper not very different from the original invoice. It will carry the heading "Credit Note" and state the amount that you owe your customer. Credit notes used to be printed in the colour red, but now businesses can print from a computer using black ink.

As with raising immediate invoices, credit notes can be raised and printed straight away. This is covered in Chapter Seven, "Generating Invoices". If you produce credit notes within another system then the transaction can be recorded in the Customer Ledger.

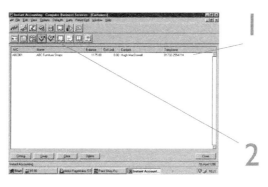

I From the Customer List window click on the customer for whom you want to issue a credit note.

2 Click on the Batch Credits icon.

REMEMBER

Look at the Customer List and it will display a new outstanding balance, the previous amount being reduced by the credit amount.

3 This input is the same as with Batch Invoices, using only the credited amount. Set the tax code (Tc) as T1 if required.

4 Click Save to post the transaction.

The Customer Statement

At the end of every month the supplier of goods may want to issue a statement to inform his customers how their account stands in his books. It will list the invoices raised that month and ensure that the customer has received them. It can also clarify certain problems should an error have occurred during that business period.

Most of us at one time or another have made a purchase on credit and you could have seen many different styles of invoices, credit notes and statements. As long as they show all the relevant details mentioned earlier, it does not matter how they are designed. Using Instant Accounting you have the option to design your own documents to suit your own needs.

Be sure to use the correct layout to fit the chosen stationery.

1 From the Customer menu, click on the Statement icon and in the next window select the required statement layout.

2 After choosing the correct layout and output options (Printer, Preview or File), click Run.

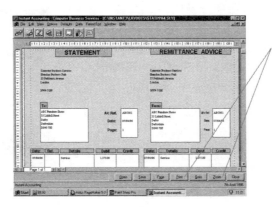

3 Click the Zoom button to zoom in or out. When satisfied click Print.

CHAPTER FIVE

The Supplier Ledger

This chapter explains the Supplier Ledger and how to create and maintain new and existing suppliers. It also covers how to analyse individual suppliers using graphs and reports.

Covers

The Supplier Record List

The second icon option on the main Instant Accounting iconbar is the Supplier (purchase) Ledger. Within this ledger you can perform the following actions:

- Maintain supplier records and their details.

- Record invoices and credit notes that you have received from your suppliers.

- Analyse your suppliers' transaction history through reports, graphs and tables.

- Generate supplier letters and mailing labels.

Once a transaction has been posted in your Supplier Record, it can no longer be deleted.

1 After clicking on the Supplier icon the Supplier desktop will appear.

2 The first icon on the left is the Supplier Record icon.

Type as many details as possible into the Supplier Record.

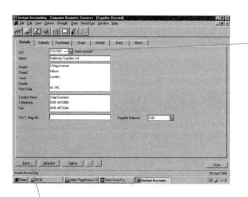

3 The Supplier Record window appears and you must enter details to create a new supplier, starting with the Account Code (A/C).

4 Click on Save to retain this information.

The Supplier Invoices

The Batch Supplier Invoices window is used to input a number of purchase transactions for which invoices have been received.

1 First move the mouse pointer over the Batch Invoices icon and click once with the left button.

2 The Batch Supplier Invoices window appears.

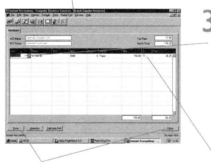

3 Type in the Supplier Account Code (A/C) or click on the Finder button just to the right of it to open the Supplier List window.

5 Click on Save, then Close.

4 Note the nominal account (N/C) default, enter a description and amount. The tax code (Tc) is automatically set at T1 (calculating VAT at 17.5%). In the case of no VAT, change this code to T9.

6 The Supplier List will display the supplier's latest balance.

The Supplier Activity

The Supplier Activity window will display the individual debit and credit entries made within a chosen supplier account. Every credit entry refers to an invoice received and every debit entry refers to an invoice paid.

1 From the Supplier List, click on the account of the supplier whose activity you want to look at.

2 Click on the Activity icon.

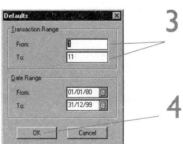

3 The next window will ask you to enter ranges for transaction numbers and/or dates.

4 Click OK.

HANDY TIP

To the far right of the Activity window, figures such as Balance, Paid and Turnover YTD (Year-to Date), can provide useful information.

5 The Supplier Activity window will be displayed. Note the credit period and the aged balance.

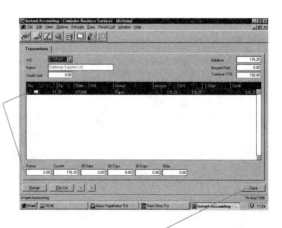

6 Click Close to finish.

The Supplier Aged Balance

Aged balances refer to the time elapsed between goods being bought and the outstanding debt to your supplier. The average period of credit given by most businesses is 30 days, but they can be negotiated to longer periods such as 60 or 90 days. Some businesses even charge interest on outstanding invoices.

1 From the Supplier List window click on the supplier for whom you want to request an aged balance.

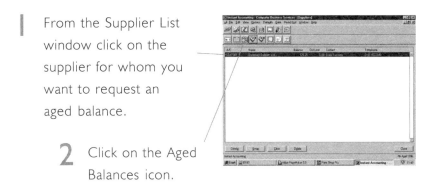

2 Click on the Aged Balances icon.

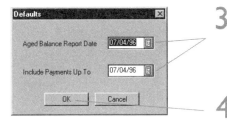

3 The next window will request a date range for required aged balances.

4 Click OK.

HANDY TIP

Click on Detailed to look up individual transactions that make up the supplier's aged balance.

5 This window will inform you of your supplier's aged balances due.

6 Click Close to finish.

The Supplier Credit Note

Sometimes when purchasing goods from your supplier, the goods could be faulty and returned to him, or the number of items dispatched could be less than you ordered.

Instead of correcting the payment due to the correct amount, you may receive a credit note from your supplier. This may be a piece of paper not very different from the original invoice. It will carry the heading "Credit Note" and state the amount that your supplier owes you. Credit notes used to be printed in the colour red, but now businesses can print from a computer using black ink.

1 From the Supplier List window click on the supplier from whom you have received a credit note.

2 Click on the Batch Credits icon.

3 This input is the same as with Batch Invoices, using only the credited amount. Set the tax code (Tc) as T1 if required.

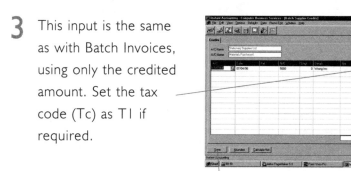

HANDY TIP

Look at the Supplier List and it will display a new outstanding balance, the previous amount being reduced by the credit amount.

4 Click Save to post the transaction.

CHAPTER SIX

The Bank

This chapter covers the maintenance of different bank accounts, and explains how to apply payments, receipts and bank transfers.

Covers

The Bank Account

Everybody will have had some sort of dealing with a bank before, probably to open an account in which to put money for safekeeping.

There are several different type of accounts in use today:

- The Current account

- The Deposit account

- The Credit Card account

- The Building Society account

The Deposit account is used for keeping your savings in one place to add to and accumulate interest payments for a period of time. This type of account is mostly used for individuals and not for business.

A Current account is preferred for business transactions. A number of cheques are supplied with this sort of account and this will be considered as the main account for your business. Although there is no interest earned with most business Current accounts, the possibility of requesting and getting an overdraft based on future business is possible.

Paying your creditors with a cheque has many advantages and avoids handling large sums of cash. Also in this world of modern technology many banks prefer to move towards electronic banking.

When you pay your creditor with a cheque, this cheque is an instruction to the bank to transfer an amount from one account to another. You, who signed the cheque, are the "drawer", and the person who goes to his bank to deposit it into his account is the "payee". His bank will present the cheque to the drawer's bank and they are called the "drawee".

...contd

The process of transferring funds takes time, called "clearing" time. This period can take anything up to four or five business days. A cheque should also be crossed with two parallel lines with the words "Account payee only". This means the amount written on the cheque can only be deposited into the payee's account. If not crossed, it is an open cheque and anybody can deposit it into their account. Most banks will supply cheques with the crossed lines already printed on them.

The Bank Accounts Window

1 Click on this icon to open the Bank Accounts window.

2 Move the mouse pointer over the required account and click once to highlight.

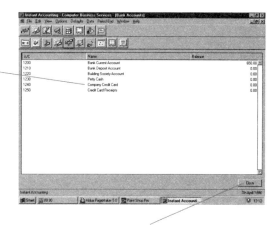

Instant Accounting treats both the Current account and Building Society account as Bank accounts.

3 Click Close to finish.

The Bank Iconbar

The Bank iconbar provides features such as account record maintenance, payments, receipts and reports.

1   Open the Bank Records.

2   Open the Bank Account Reconciliation.

3   Make a Bank Payment.

4   Make a Supplier Payment.

 Move the mouse pointer over the required icon and the description will display itself.

5   Enter a Receipt.

6   Enter a Customer Receipt.

7   Enter an Account Transfer.

8   Enter Recurring Entries.

9   Run the Bank Statement.

10   Run Bank Account Reports.

Setting Up Bank Account Details

 | Click on this icon to enter account record details.

 REMEMBER

When setting up your own Bank account use nominal codes 1200 to 1299.

2 Make any necessary changes here.

3 Click on the Bank Details tab.

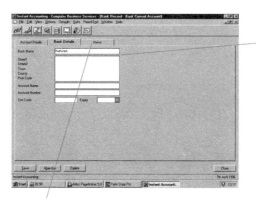

4 Enter all necessary Bank account details here.

5 Click on the Memo tab next.

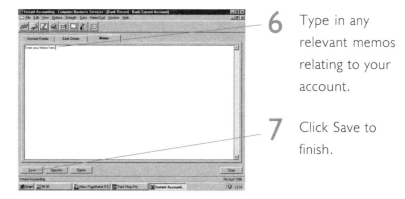

6 Type in any relevant memos relating to your account.

7 Click Save to finish.

Recording Bank Payments

The Bank Payment option should only be used for payments other than supplier payments, being any payments made against lodged invoices. For these you should use the Supplier Payments screen.

1 Move the mouse pointer over the required account and click once.

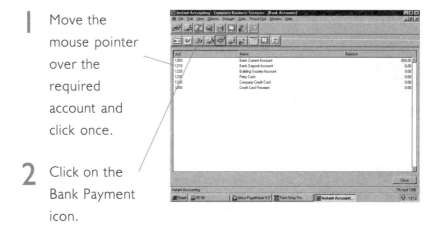

2 Click on the Bank Payment icon.

Use the Calendar button to enter the date.

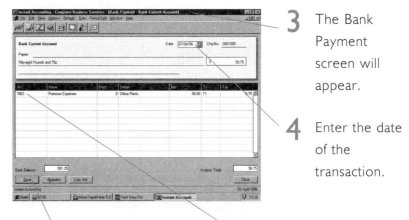

3 The Bank Payment screen will appear.

4 Enter the date of the transaction.

6 Click Save to post the transaction.

5 Enter the correct nominal code and then all details such as description, amount and tax code.

Credit Card Transactions

More businesses will make payments using their business credit card. Use the Credit Card account already set up for those transactions.

1 Move the mouse pointer over the Credit Card account and click once to highlight.

You can also post credit card payments using the Bank Current account. See Recording Bank Payments.

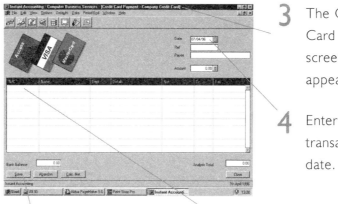

2 Click on the Payment icon.

3 The Credit Card Payment screen will appear.

4 Enter the transaction date.

6 Click Save to post the transaction

5 Choose the correct nominal code and then enter all necessary details such as description, amount and tax code.

Cash Accounts

This section is about the Cash account, more commonly known as Petty Cash. This account is a subdivision of your Bank account and is listed within your Bank option.

What is Petty Cash? On a daily basis the business may have a number of small miscellaneous expenses, such as tea and coffee or office stationery. Instead of issuing a bank cheque for such small amounts, a designated employee of the company usually controls the Petty Cash box.

In it is kept a small amount of cash to cover those particular expenses. The returned receipt for the purchase is then recorded in the Petty Cash book or, in your case, in the Payment screen within the Petty Cash account.

On a regular basis, maybe once a month, a cheque is then raised to replenish the Petty Cash box and is recorded as a Bank Account Transfer, covered in a later section of this chapter.

1 Move the mouse pointer over the Petty Cash account and click once to highlight.

2 Click on the Payment icon.

Cash Account Payment & Receipt

Cash Payments

This screen is used to enter individual Petty Cash expenses.

1 Enter a reference.

2 Enter the transaction date.

HANDY TIP

Use the Calendar button to enter the date.

3 Choose the correct Nominal Expense account code.

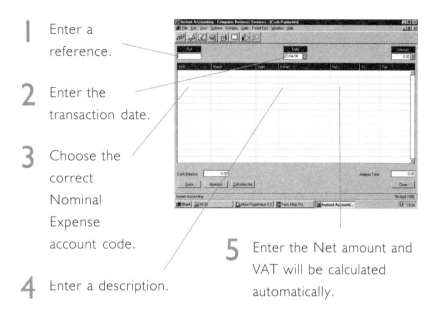

4 Enter a description.

5 Enter the Net amount and VAT will be calculated automatically.

Cash Receipts

Sometimes a business will deal a lot in cash, not just using Petty Cash. This is when a Cash account can be used, for example, for depositing cash in a night safe. When receiving cash the Cash Receipts window should be used, followed by an Account Transfer when the cash is deposited into the Current account.

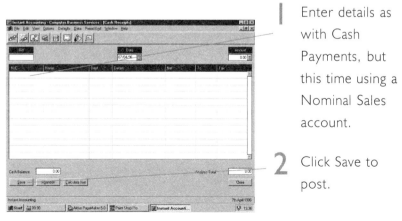

1 Enter details as with Cash Payments, but this time using a Nominal Sales account.

2 Click Save to post.

Supplier Payments

The Supplier Payment is your payment on account. The transaction of the goods purchased has already been made by entering the invoice details into the Supplier Ledger.

| Click on Bank Current Account.

2 Click on the Supplier Payment icon.

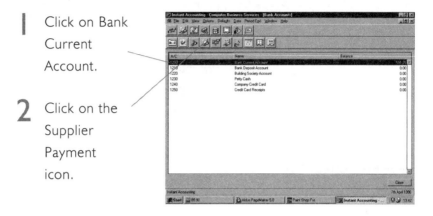

3 The Supplier Payment screen will appear.

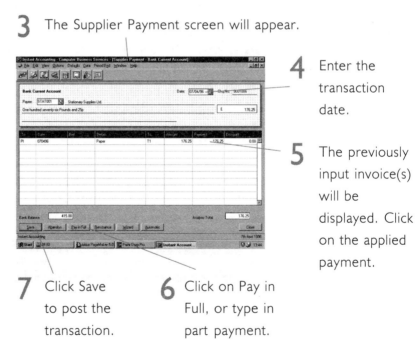

4 Enter the transaction date.

5 The previously input invoice(s) will be displayed. Click on the applied payment.

7 Click Save to post the transaction.

6 Click on Pay in Full, or type in part payment.

Bank Receipt

The Bank Receipt option should only be used for receipts not including customer receipts, meaning any receipts pertaining to lodged invoices within the Customer Ledger.

1 Click on Bank Current Account.

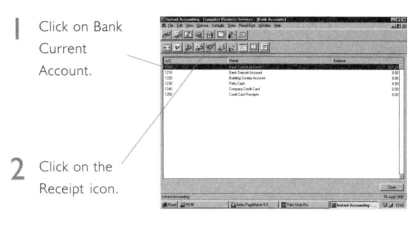

HANDY TIP

Enter the total amount in the Amount box to act as a check that all individual payments have been entered.

2 Click on the Receipt icon.

3 The Bank Receipt window will appear.

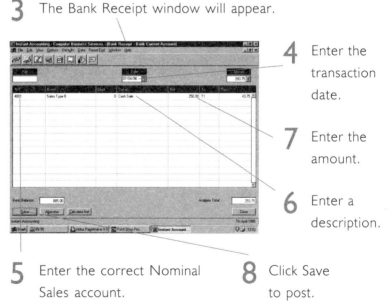

4 Enter the transaction date.

7 Enter the amount.

6 Enter a description.

5 Enter the correct Nominal Sales account.

8 Click Save to post.

Customer Receipt

The Customer Receipt is your receipt on account. The transaction of the goods sold has already been entered by posting the invoice details into the Customer Ledger.

1 Click on Bank Current Account.

2 Click on the Customer Receipt icon.

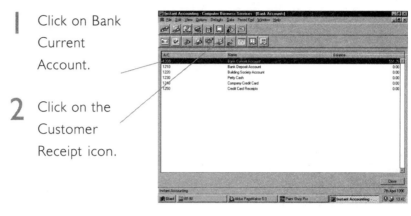

You can use the Automatic button to allocate full payment to all outstanding payments.

3 The Customer Receipt window will appear.

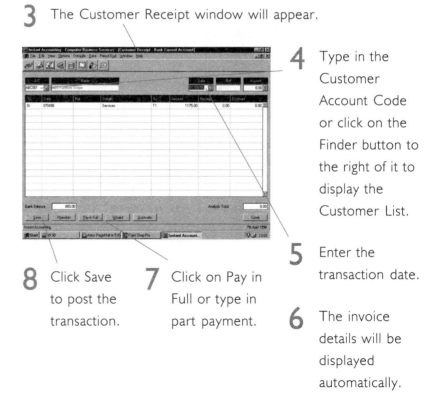

4 Type in the Customer Account Code or click on the Finder button to the right of it to display the Customer List.

8 Click Save to post the transaction.

7 Click on Pay in Full or type in part payment.

5 Enter the transaction date.

6 The invoice details will be displayed automatically.

The Bank Account Transfer

As the heading implies, this option is used to transfer money between Bank accounts.

1 Click on Bank Current Account.

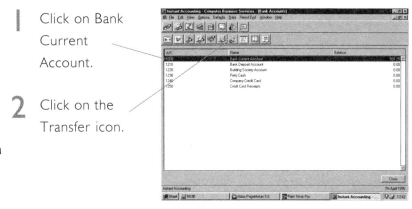

2 Click on the Transfer icon.

REMEMBER

This option will only transfer values between Bank accounts, and there is no VAT included.

3 The Transfer window will appear.

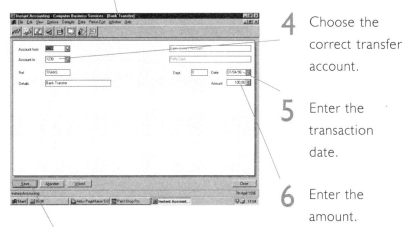

4 Choose the correct transfer account.

5 Enter the transaction date.

6 Enter the amount.

HANDY TIP

Use the Calendar button to enter the date.

7 Click Save to post the transaction.

Recurring Entries

Every month it is necessary to check recurring entries within the bank statement, such as direct debits and standing orders. They can be easily forgotten, and the Recurring Entries screen will remind you. It will display itself when the program starts if you wish it to do so.

Click on the Recurring Entries icon and then the Add button to start new entries.

REMEMBER

Instant Accounting will only let you post a journal credit with the corresponding journal debit or vice versa.

1 Choose either Payment or Receipt.

2 Choose the correct Bank account.

3 Enter the Nominal Code.

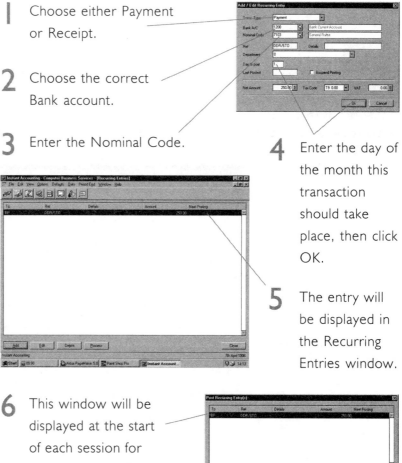

4 Enter the day of the month this transaction should take place, then click OK.

5 The entry will be displayed in the Recurring Entries window.

6 This window will be displayed at the start of each session for you to process the recurring entry.

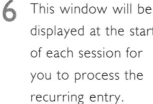

The Bank Account Reconciliation

At regular intervals when you receive your bank statements you should check the bank's records with your own, comparing all transactions. This procedure is called reconciling your bank account in your books with what the bank has recorded.

It could be that you have not as yet posted the bank charges or some direct debits. But even if you have, the two balances will no doubt be different from each other. The reason for this is that some cheque payments to your suppliers have not yet been presented to your bank and therefore do not show in your statement.

You may have already posted the payment in the Bank Supplier Payment section, and that posting would have changed your bank balance in Instant Accounting. If that payment was not presented by the time the statement was printed then the two account balances will differ.

Once you have assured yourself that any outstanding transactions have been made you can click on the Bank Reconciliation icon in the Bank window. Every bank transaction made will appear in front of you, and using the bank statement you can highlight them one at a time if they have also been transacted by your bank.

1 Choose the account to be reconciled.

2 Click on the Bank Account Reconciliation icon.

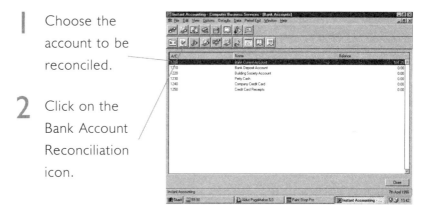

...contd

The Bank Account Reconciliation

At the bottom of the Bank Reconciliation screen a bank and book balance will appear. Once all transactions have been reconciled, the statement balance in the Reconciliation window should be the same as the balance on your bank statement. This assures you that all transactions concerning your Bank account have been made.

Only those transactions not previously reconciled will appear.

1 Click on the transaction as in the bank statement.

2 The selected transaction will be highlighted.

3 Check the Book and Statement Balances.

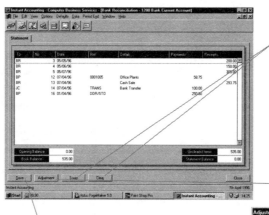

4 Click Swap to highlight all transactions or Clear to deselect all.

5 Make any adjustments to transactions.

Bank transactions will show an R when reconciled and an N when not reconciled within the Audit Trail.

7 Click Save when finished.

6 Enter the required details of the adjustment.

The Bank Statement

At regular intervals your bank will supply you with a copy of your account from their Customer Ledger, showing all transactions made in your account since the last statement.

After you have finished reconciling your Bank accounts you can print your own bank statements for one or all of them, showing all reconciled transactions. That printed statement should match the statement provided by your bank.

I Choose the account you want a statement for.

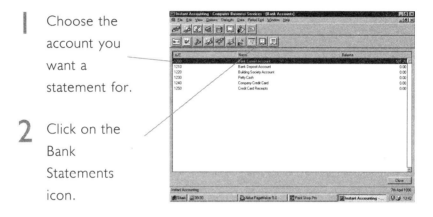

2 Click on the Bank Statements icon.

3 The Bank Statements window will appear.

HANDY TIP

Use the Calendar button to enter the date.

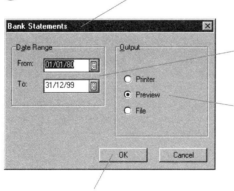

4 Enter the date range for the required statement.

5 Choose the required output.

6 Click OK to run the report.

The Bank Reports

Start the Bank Reports option by clicking on the Reports icon on the Bank iconbar. There are already a large number of predesigned reports available that should cover most of your needs.

1 Click on the Bank Reports icon.

2 Choose the required report.

HANDY TIP

Use the Preview option to ensure you have selected the correct report.

3 Choose the required output.

4 Click on Run.

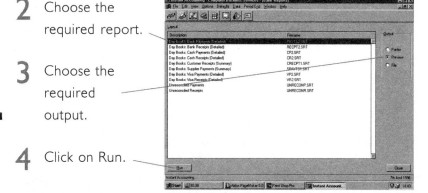

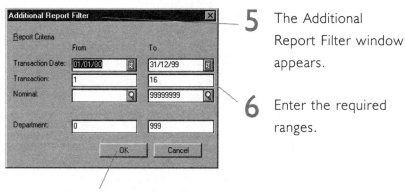

5 The Additional Report Filter window appears.

6 Enter the required ranges.

7 Click here to run the report.

CHAPTER SEVEN

Generating Invoices

This chapter explains how to generate and print invoices and credit notes.

Covers

Stock

Stock is comprised of purchased materials that are intended for resale. You purchase items from a number of suppliers to resell them or to manufacture new products from them. The general idea is to purchase at a certain price and resell at a marked-up price to create a gross profit.

Stock levels will fluctuate on a daily basis and at the end of set accounting periods you count what stock there is on hand. This is commonly known as making a "stocktake". Because those stock levels change within a twelve-month period, stock is referred to as a current asset.

If you were to sell your stock at the same price as you bought it then it would be easy to account for it. You would debit the value of your purchase from your supplier and credit the sale. The balance of the account would then represent the cost of the goods unsold. But if you did that then you wouldn't be in business for very long.

It is not possible to record the cost of the goods and the sales price in the same account since the balance would not represent the cost of the goods purchased. Therefore you use two separate accounts to record purchases and sales.

The Product Record

Instant Accounting has a Products option. There you can maintain product records and use those details when generating a product invoice.

1 From the main desktop select the Products icon.

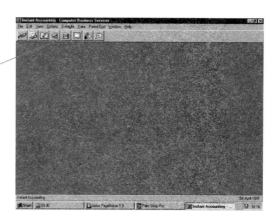

2 Move the mouse pointer over the Record icon and click once to create your first product records.

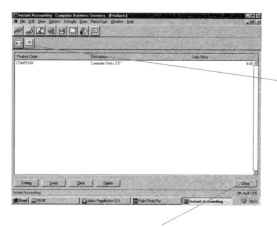

3 Click Close to finish.

Product Record Details

With this option you can create individual product records.

1 Enter a product code.

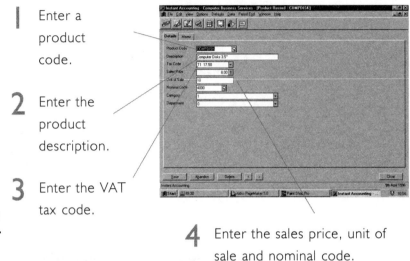

2 Enter the product description.

To move between tab dialogs press Ctrl + Page Up or Ctrl + Page Down.

3 Enter the VAT tax code.

4 Enter the sales price, unit of sale and nominal code.

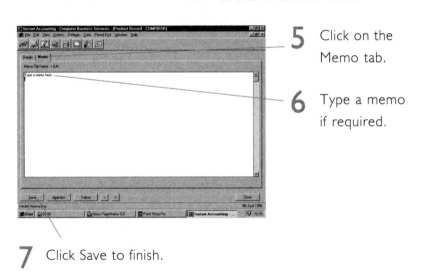

5 Click on the Memo tab.

6 Type a memo if required.

7 Click Save to finish.

The Invoice Iconbar

The Invoice iconbar provides features such as product and service invoice generation, credit note generation, the printing of invoices and updating of ledgers.

1   Create a Product Invoice.

2   Create a Service Invoice.

 Move the mouse pointer over the required icon and the description will display itself.

3   Create a Product Credit Note.

4   Create a Service Credit Note.

5   Print Invoices and Credit Notes.

6   Update the Ledgers.

7   Run Invoice Reports.

The Product Invoice

When you want to record a purchase transaction concerning goods intended for resale, you must consider two different types of categories – cash and credit purchases. In the case of a cash transaction, where goods were paid for straight away, you must debit the Purchase account and credit the Cash or Bank account. In most cases, however, a business will arrange to purchase its goods for resale on account from its suppliers. This can be any period between 30 and 120 days. Therefore, once goods are purchased your business has incurred a debt and your suppliers have become your creditors.

At the same time you may sell goods to your customers on account and in this case they become your debtors. The double-entry consists of a credit entry in your Sales account and a debit entry in your Cash or Bank account in the case of an immediate sale.

When a sale on account is being transacted, an invoice must be raised informing the recipient of his or her debt.

1 Move the mouse pointer over the Invoice icon.

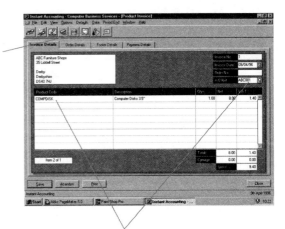

2 In the Invoices window, click on the Product Invoice icon.

3 Enter the required customer account code. Continue by entering the invoice number, date, and product items.

The Service Invoice

If your business is in the service industry then you may want to use the Service Invoice, rather than the Product Invoice option. There is as much room as you need to enter text; all other options, such as Nominal Code and price, can be entered individually.

1 First open the Invoicing window.

2 Move the cursor over the Service Invoice icon and click once.

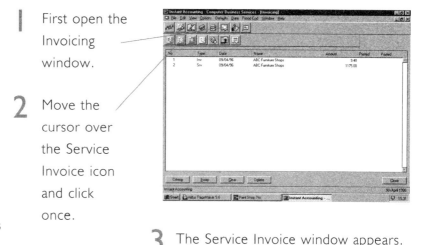

HANDY TIP

The customer's address will be displayed automatically. It can be changed if necessary, but it will not change the Customer Record.

3 The Service Invoice window appears.

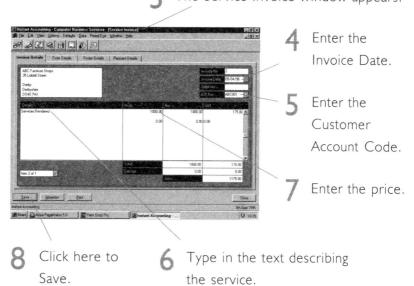

4 Enter the Invoice Date.

5 Enter the Customer Account Code.

7 Enter the price.

8 Click here to Save.

6 Type in the text describing the service.

Generating Credit Notes

Sometimes when you forward goods to your customer some of them could be faulty and they are returned to you. Or the number of items dispatched might be less than stated on the invoice.

Instead of correcting the payment to the true amount you may issue a credit note. This may be a piece of paper not very different from the original invoice. It will carry the heading "Credit Note" instead of "Invoice" and state the amount that you owe your customer. Credit notes used to be printed in the colour red, but now businesses can print from a computer using black ink.

Generating a Product or Service credit note is very similar to generating an invoice, keeping in mind that the value transacted is money returned to the customer.

1   Click on the Product Credit Note or Service Credit Note icon.

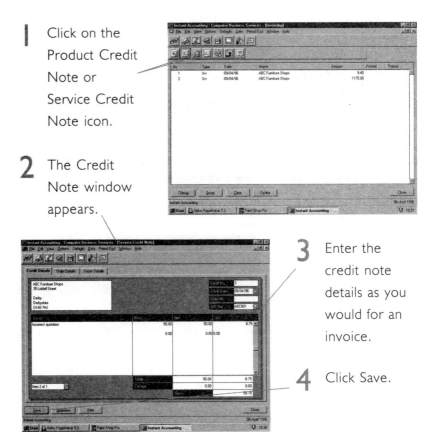

HANDY TIP

You can reprint your invoices and credit notes as many times as needed.

2   The Credit Note window appears.

3   Enter the credit note details as you would for an invoice.

4   Click Save.

Printing Invoices

Each individual invoice created can be printed straight away. Alternatively, if you have to enter a large number of invoices in one go you can use the Print Batch Invoices option. Once the invoices have been printed the output should be checked for any errors. Printing the invoices will not update the ledgers, so if errors occur you can change the invoice.

Instant Accounting will display a warning if you try to change invoices that have already been posted.

| Move the mouse pointer over the Print Invoices icon and click once.

2 The Print Invoice window will appear. With the cursor select the required invoice file.

3 Select the required output.

4 Run the print job.

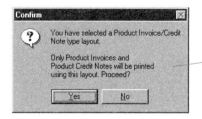

5 Instant Accounting will request confirmation that you have chosen the correct layout file.

Updating the Ledgers

Once all invoices have been generated and printed and you are satisfied that all the details on them are correct, you have to update the ledgers by posting the transactions into the Customer and Nominal Ledgers.

If you change any invoice details after you update the ledgers it will not include them within the ledgers.

1 You may want to select individual invoices first.

2 Select all invoices to be posted by clicking on them once.

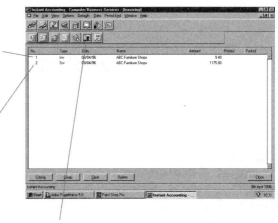

3 Click on the Update Ledgers icon and then choose the required output.

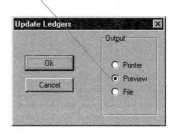

4 Preview the update report if you want to change aspects of the layout, such as paper size, orientation and margins.

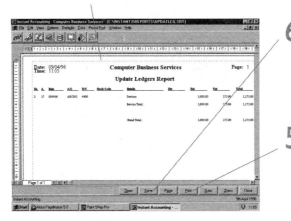

6 Click Save if you want to keep the report.

5 Click here if you want to print the report.

Deleting Invoices

You may decide to delete the generated invoices after the ledgers have been updated. This will not reverse the postings. When you delete unposted invoices you should use the Compress Data Files option within Oops! to conserve disk space.

1 In the Invoicing window move the mouse pointer over the invoice you want to delete and click once.

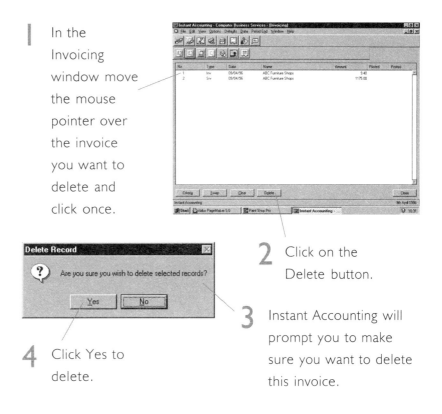

2 Click on the Delete button.

3 Instant Accounting will prompt you to make sure you want to delete this invoice.

4 Click Yes to delete.

Invoice Reports

Start the Invoice Reports option by clicking the Reports icon on the Invoice iconbar. There are already three predesigned reports available that should cover most of your needs.

 | Click on the Invoice Reports icon.

2 Choose the required report.

3 Choose the required output.

4 Click Run to print the report.

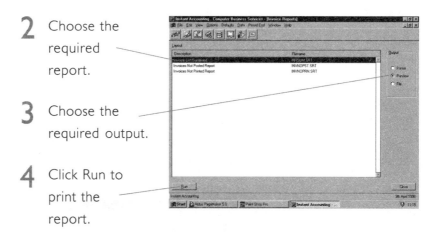

CHAPTER EIGHT

Financials

This chapter explains how to generate your management reports and VAT return. It also explains how to read and interpret your management reports.

Covers

The Financials Iconbar

The Financials iconbar will open the following reporting procedures:

1   Open the Audit Trail report.

2   Open the Trial Balance report.

 Move the mouse pointer over the required icon and the description will display itself.

3   Open the Profit & Loss statement.

4   Open the Balance Sheet report.

5   Open the Budget report.

6   Open the Prior Year report.

7   Open the VAT Return.

Net Worth

When the Balance Sheet was discussed, it was said that it will inform you of your business's financial situation – in other words, it will tell you what it is worth at a certain time. You may have already thought of the next formula by deducing that when you take the value of your assets and subtract the value of your liabilities you should be left with the difference. This is called "Net Worth", and the equation looks like this:

Net Value of the business = Assets - Liabilities

Once you create a profit in a certain business period you will ultimately end up with more money in the till. So how is this "Net Profit" accounted for?

Remember the chair you bought at the auction, restored and then sold for £90? That day you made a net profit of £20. There was a total outlay of £70, which was your Capital.

Once you sold the chair it changed from being an asset to a profit, which you can use in a number of ways. For the time being, however, it will be recorded below your capital. Before you had £70, and now you have £90. You reinvest that £90 into the business. It could be said that it is part of your capital, but it will not leave the business's entity and therefore will be recorded separately, below the capital.

Capital + Profit = Assets - Liabilities

Capital & Revenue Expenditure

So far we have considered how double-entry bookkeeping works, and in this chapter we are going to take this a step further. It was mentioned that the reason for keeping a record of all your business transactions is to be able to collate management reports that will inform you of how your business is performing at any given time.

The Balance Sheet has already been covered in some length. Before analysing this and the reports in greater detail, we must discuss what is displayed in each, and how this information is derived. Therefore we will talk more about accounting principles and conventions.

The concept of gross and net profit has also been covered, and we have defined values such as the total income or revenue earned, less the cost of sales and expenditures incurred by the business. If the total revenue is greater than the purchases then you have made a profit; if not, then a loss has been incurred.

There is at least one time when you will have to prepare business accounts and statements, and that is at the end of your financial year. Your accountant will audit those records as an independent party on behalf of the Inland Revenue and present the final output to the Inspector of Taxes.

So let us start with capital expenditure, which is expenditure incurred in acquiring or improving fixed assets. This can include improvements on property or the acquisition of a motor vehicle.

On the other hand, revenue expenditure is expenditure incurred in the normal day-to-day running of the business, and covers all expenditures not covered as a purchase or improvement of a fixed asset.

Capital & Revenue Income

Capital income is finance invested in a business either by the owner or from an outside source such as a bank. If the owner invests in his or her business it is usually intended to be for a period longer than three months and therefore is treated as capital.

Revenue is income earned by the business from normal trading activities. Remember, you are in business to create maximised profits, and to be able to achieve this in a certain accounting period your revenue must be more than your expenditures. Revenue income is created by the sale of goods or services that your business trades in.

Provisions & Reserves

Should the situation arise that a customer is unable to pay for his or her debt, that value becomes a bad debt and you will have to credit the Debtors Control account and debit the Bad Debt account. The Profit & Loss account will adjust accordingly to cover this revenue expense.

But sometimes it is impossible for you to know that you will incur a bad debt, particularly if it happens to fall in the next accounting period.

In order to provide for such circumstances when it comes to preparing the final accounts you can create "Reserves" or "Provisions".

When you have made a net profit in your final accounts some of it may be transferred to a "Reserves" account. This part of the profit is not intended for distribution and is used for a possible future event. Reserves may be used for a specific purpose or a general expense, such as the upgrading of a fixed asset, or to cover an unknown event.

On the other hand, "Provisions" are intended to cover such expenses as bad debts or other costs incurred through normal business activities. Your accountant will be able to assist you in working out the amounts used to cover Provisions and Reserves. The percentages are based on past experience of the amount of bad debts incurred.

The Audit Trail

When you first click on the Financials icon the Audit Trail window will appear, displaying the latest transactions. You can scroll back as far as there are transactions and as long as they have not been cleared by the Month End procedure.

It is called the Audit Trail because it is a report that is often requested by your auditors at the end of the year. This report will show every transaction ever made, in numerical order. In the reporting procedure there are options available to define a brief or detailed report. It is recommended that after every posting session you print out a session report, forming an Audit Trail using the Filter options and entering the date of your session.

If you do clear the Audit Trail at the end of the month, you should always make a backup and print out the month's transactions before running the Month End procedure. Instant Accounting can store up to 2,000,000,000 transactions, and providing you have enough system resources, you should never have to clear the Audit Trail. But it can slow down your system when Instant Accounting is trying to extract transactions to process reports.

HANDY TIP

Maximise the Financials window to display as many transactions of the Audit Trail as possible, then use the scroll bar to display more transactions.

1 Click on the Financials icon.

2 The Audit Trail will appear.

3 Scroll the window to display previous transactions.

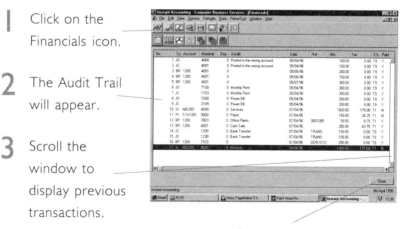

4 Click Close to finish.

The Audit Trail is a very detailed report. The column "Tp" identifies what type each individual transaction is. Here are the different codes:

- BR – Bank Receipt
- BP – Bank Payment
- CP – Cash Payment
- CR – Cash Receipt
- JD – Journal Debit
- JC – Journal Credit
- SI – Sales Invoice
- SR – Sales Receipt
- SC – Sales Credit Note
- SA – Sales Receipt on Account
- PI – Purchase Invoice
- PP – Purchase Payment
- PC – Purchase Credit Note
- PA – Purchase Payment on Account

 | Click on the Audit Trail icon.

2 Choose the report type.

3 Choose the required output.

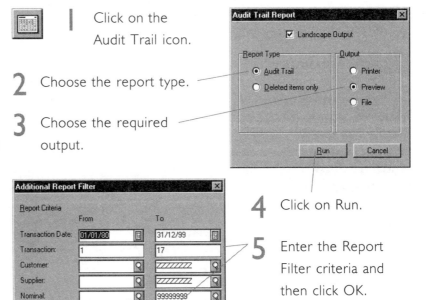

REMEMBER

Be as detailed as possible with your customer and/or supplier account codes input.

4 Click on Run.

5 Enter the Report Filter criteria and then click OK.

The Trial Balance

When you click on the Trial Balance icon in the Financials window, the program will extract all accounts that hold a debit or credit value. It will not use accounts with a zero balance.

The Trial Balance is particularly useful when checking the output of management reports or VAT Liability reports. All Liability accounts should show a credit balance and all Asset accounts a debit balance. Also, the Sales accounts should show a credit balance and the Purchase and Expense accounts a debit balance.

At the bottom the totals of the debit and credit columns are displayed, and they should always balance. If they do not then an error has occurred and this has to be investigated. It could mean the management reports are incorrect.

1 Click on the Trial Balance icon.

2 Choose the required period.

3 Choose the required output.

4 Click on Run.

5 Preview first to check the layout and then print.

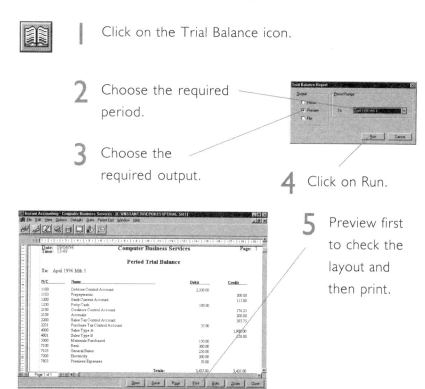

The Profit & Loss Report

The Profit & Loss statement is without doubt the most important management report. It will show how the business has performed within a certain accounting period. It will start with the values of the Sales accounts within the Nominal Ledger and continue with all other accounts that have been entered in the Chart of Accounts layout.

After adding the sales values it will deduct the purchase values (from Nominal account 5000) and then the Direct Expenses accounts (up to 6999). This will produce the gross profit or loss.

It will then continue to extract the values of the Overhead accounts (from Nominal account 7000). Subtracting the cumulative amount of those overheads from the gross profit or loss amount, it will calculate the net profit or loss.

1   Click on the Profit & Loss icon.

2   Choose the required period.

3   Choose the required output.

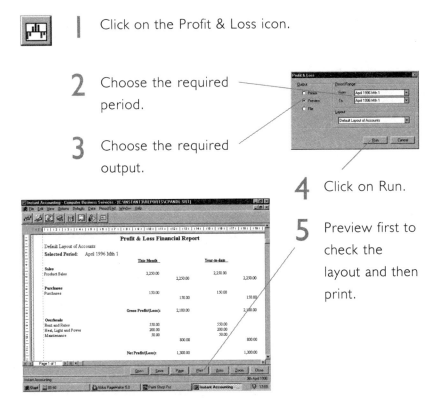

4   Click on Run.

5   Preview first to check the layout and then print.

The Balance Sheet

The Balance Sheet is not an account as such, but is included as a final report, as it is drawn at the end of the financial period.

The Report program only extracts values from the Asset and Liability accounts within the Chart of Accounts. The Fixed Asset accounts range from 0001 to 0999, the Current Asset accounts from 1000 to 1999, the Liability accounts from 2000 to 2999 and the Capital accounts from 3000 to 3999.

HANDY TIP

Make sure before running the Balance Sheet Report that the depreciation, prepayments and accruals have been posted when running the Month End procedure.

The traditional method of displaying the Balance Sheet used to be a left-to-right layout, with the assets on the left (debit entries) and the liabilities and capital on the right (credit entries). Instant Accounting adopts the more modern layout, this being from top to bottom. The Fixed and Current assets come first, and are then reduced by the Liabilities. That balance should equal the Capital balance.

This conforms to the following accounting equation:

Fixed + Current Assets - Liabilities = Capital

| | 1 | Click on the Balance Sheet icon. |

2 Choose the required period and output.

REMEMBER

It is a good idea to check the Asset and Liability accounts in the Trial Balance when producing the Balance Sheet.

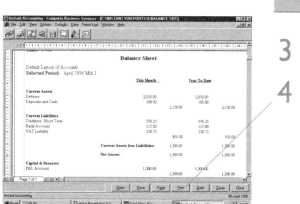

3 Click on Run.

4 Preview first to check the layout and then print.

Gross & Net Ratio

Once the final reports have been produced, you may want to determine the relationship that exists between the presented figures. We call this process "ratios", highlighting those figures to be able to predict future trends and base sound management decisions on them.

In previous chapters we have already discussed how we come to gross and net profit. The gross profit ratio is determined by dividing the gross profit by the sales figures.

For example, if the gross profit stands at £40,000 and the sales turnover is £80,000 then the gross profit ratio is 50% ((40,000 / 80,000) x 100).

The net profit ratio is calculated in a similar way and expressed as a percentage. If the business's net profit is £10,000 then the net profit ratio would be 12.5% ((10,000 / 80,000) x 100).

As you may have already noted, ratios are listed in the Prior Year report. The reason for this is that ratios are used to determine a relationship between two different accounting periods.

Gross and net profit ratios will show how well the business has performed. The above example has shown a 12.5% net profit ratio; in the next accounting period the sales have gone up to £100,000 and the net profit is £12,000. The net profit ratio for the second period is 12%. Although the sales have increased in the second period, the expenses have been higher and the ratio is less than in the first period.

Thus, the ratio informs you that sales turnover has increased, but that the overall business performance has decreased for the second accounting period. The reason for this will have to be looked into.

Stock Turnover Ratio

Stock, of course, can have a great effect on the gross profit. Stock that is lying on the shelves for long periods is not turned into sales revenue and therefore reduces gross profit. The stock turnover ratio will determine the average stock held within a certain accounting period.

Let us say that the total sales figure is £80,000, the opening stock is £20,000 and the closing stock is £15,000. At the end of every accounting period a stock-take is performed, informing you of the opening and closing stock figures. The above figures will give the average stock held for that accounting period as £17,500 ((20,000 + 15,000) / 2). The stock turnover ratio is 4.57 (80,000 / 17,500).

That ratio tells you that your business is turning stock over 4.57 times during that accounting period. If your accounting period is monthly then this could also be expressed as stock being turned over every 6.8 days in a 31-day accounting period (31 days / 4.57).

Hence it is advantageous to try to increase the stock turnover ratio to increase the sales and prevent tying cash up in held stock.

Current & Liquid Ratio

The current ratio is calculated from the value of current assets and liabilities to determine the difference, which is also known as working capital. Hence the current ratio is also sometimes referred to as the "working capital ratio".

For example, the value of the business's current assets is £100,000 and the value of its liabilities is £45,000. Therefore the current ratio stands at 2.22 (100,000/ 45,000). Alternatively, one might say that the business's current assets will cover its liabilities 2.22 times, the business's working capital being £55,000. This is a very good indicator to show that the business can pay off the liabilities, should they fall due, without having to touch any of the fixed assets.

But it would not be a good idea to have too high a current ratio, because that would mean that your current assets were too high, too much cash being tied up in stock or the Debtors Control account. That can also create another problem should the business show high balances in the Stock and Debtors accounts and on the other hand a low bank balance. If all liabilities fall due it may be difficult to turn current stock values into cash quickly, and it may take time for your debtors to come forth with outstanding payments.

The liquid ratio is an extension of the current ratio. Because it is mainly concerned with available cash or current assets that may be turned into cash quickly (i.e., liquid assets), it is also referred to as the quick ratio. This ratio will show how the business is able to cover its liabilities without including stock.

Debtors & Creditors Ratio

The debtors ratio is determined by dividing the annual Trade Debtors value by the value of Total Credit Sales. This time we do not express the outcome as a percentage, but as a timed period.

If the value of trade debtors for the accounting period is £28,000 and the value of total sales is £350,000 then the ratio is 4.16 weeks ((28,000 / 350,000) x 52 weeks).

This tells us that it takes your debtors an average of 4.16 weeks to clear their debt. It is in your business's interest to keep this ratio as low as possible, meaning to turn your credit sales into cash quickly.

The creditors ratio, on the other hand, will tell you how quickly your business pays its own debts and hence reduces your Bank account asset. The annual Trade Creditors value is divided by the total value of credit purchases, the outcome again being a timed period.

Ideally, you should minimise the debtors ratio and maximise the creditors ratio to optimum level, keeping in mind such things as valued customer relations and supplier discount offers.

The Budget Report

1 Click on the Budget Analysis icon.

2 Choose the required period.

3 Choose the required output.

4 Click on Run.

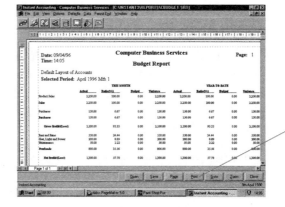

5 Preview first to check the layout and then print.

The Prior Year Report

As with the Budget Report, this output will show the values of the Sales, Purchase, Direct Expenses and Overhead accounts. It will show the current month or selected period and also the year-to-date figures and compare them with the figures of the previous year.

Again, each account will display the ratios calculated as in the Budget Report. This will give you a clear picture of how the business is performing in relation to the previous year.

1   Click on the Prior Year icon.

2   Choose the required period.

3   Choose the required output.

4   Click on Run.

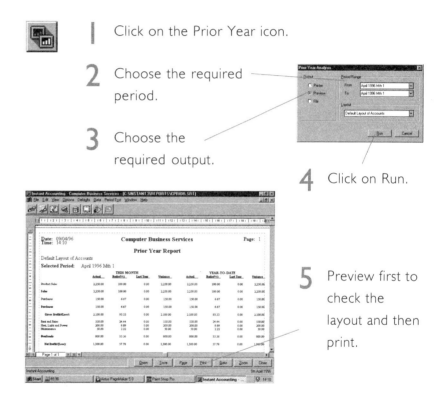

5   Preview first to check the layout and then print.

The VAT Return

VAT is an important tax liability that many businesses are concerned with. If your business has an annual turnover of a certain amount, set yearly in the Budget, then your business must be registered with Customs & Excise.

If that is the case then Customs & Excise will provide you with a VAT number, which must be noted in all correspondence with your clients, and which will inform them that you collect VAT on behalf of Customs & Excise.

Value Added Tax is ultimately charged to the final consumer who purchases goods or services. If your business purchases certain vatable goods for the reason of reselling them then your business is not the final consumer and VAT paid can be reclaimed.

Those goods or services including VAT purchased by the business are called *input* tax. When you invoice your customer and add VAT to the price of your goods or services, this is called *output* tax.

At the time of writing the standard VAT was set at 17.5%. Therefore, any goods or services bought or sold that include VAT will have 17.5% added to their net value.

In the Nominal Ledger of Instant Accounting you may have noted three accounts called Sales Tax Control account, Purchase Tax Control account and VAT Liability account. When an invoice that includes VAT is posted, that value is posted to the appropriate Tax Control account, depending on whether it was a sale or a purchase.

The accumulated amounts in the Sales account comprise your *output* tax, and the balance in the Purchase account is your *input* tax.

Every three months Customs & Excise requires you to send in the VAT Return informing them of the value of your *input* and *output* taxes. When you run the VAT Return program in the Financials window, all that is required of you is to enter the process dates of the required period. The program will then calculate the difference between your *input* and *output* taxes. That difference will tell you if money is due to be paid to Customs & Excise or if money is to be paid to your business by them.

Once you are satisfied that the figures are correct, the value of sales and purchase tax should be journalised out of the Control accounts and the difference posted into the VAT Liability account. Finally, when the bank payment to Customs & Excise is made or received, the same amount will then balance the VAT Liability account, leaving a zero balance.

Ensure that you enter the correct date range for the VAT Return. If not correct, the output from Instant Accounting will also be incorrect.

1 Click on the VAT Return icon in the Financials window.

2 The VAT Return window will appear.

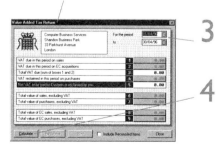

3 Enter the start and end dates of the required VAT Return.

4 Click the Calculate button.

...contd

The VAT Return program will run through the Audit Trail to check all vatable transactions. This means that your original input will have to be correct. Sometimes, however, errors occur. This is why every time you run a VAT Return it is advisable to make a manual check and reconcile the accounts. This will ensure that nothing has been missed.

 It is important to reconcile the Control accounts and to check your Audit Trail before you run the VAT Return.

| After you click the Calculate button Instant Accounting will inform you of the amount of VAT transactions made within that period.

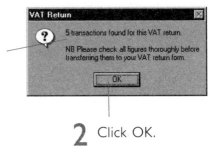

2 Click OK.

3 It is possible to analyse the breakdown of the VAT Return. Click on any of the VAT value total buttons.

 Once you are satisfied that the VAT Return is correct, print it and click the Reconcile button.

4 The VAT Breakdown appears.

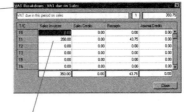

5 Double-click on an individual tax code total for a further breakdown.

CHAPTER NINE

Period End

This chapter explains how to run the Month End and Year End procedures, how to clear the Audit Trail and how to calculate depreciation.

Covers

The Month End Procedure

At the end of every month you should close off your month's transaction history by reconciling the accounts. Transactions such as prepayments and accruals have to be processed, and the Fixed Asset accounts will have to be changed by posting the depreciations.

If your business performs many transactions within a month's period, you might want to clear the Audit Trail.

You will be able to post transactions dated before or after the period once the Month End procedure has been run.

Starting Month End

1. Make sure you have posted all transactions for that month.

2. Process all recurring entries.

3. Have all prepayments and accruals posted.

4. Check for any new Fixed Asset accounts.

5. Reconcile the Bank account.

6. Print all necessary product reports.

Continue with the following procedure:

Don't forget to back up your data and change the program date to the last day of the calendar month.

It is very likely that you want to run the Month End procedure on a day other than the last calendar day of the month. This is why you must change the program date first.

1 Back up your data files.

2 From the Instant Accounting menu bar click on Defaults.

3 Click on Change Program Date.

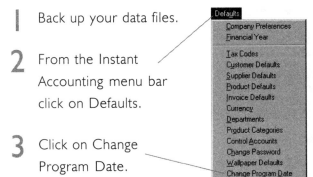

4 From the Instant Accounting menu bar click on Period End.

5 Click on the Month End option.

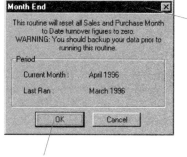

6 The Month End processing window will appear.

7 Make sure you posted your prepayments, accruals and depreciation using the Journal before running Month End.

8 Click OK to start the Month End procedure.

After the Month End program has finished another backup should be made (see Chapter Eleven, "Data Management", for backup procedures). It is best to keep a number of generations of your backup data files, with one copy on-site and another off-site for security reasons.

Finally, you can print the Management (financial) Reports, such as the Profit & Loss statement, Balance Sheet, Aged Debtors and Creditors Analysis Reports and the Trial Balance. You may also want to run the Oops! option to compress any data files.

Depreciation

It was noted before that capital expenditure and income should not be included in the Profit & Loss statement because they are intended to hold their value for a period of twelve months or longer; whereas revenue expenditure and income will fluctuate within a twelve-month period. The Chart of Accounts has a logical layout, the first half of which covers Asset, Liability and Capital accounts, all relating to capital expenditure and income.

However, when you purchase or improve assets you know that they will not hold their value forever, and that at the end of twelve months, were you to sell those assets, you would receive less money for them than what you paid for them in the first place.

For that reason the value that is being used up during that twelve-month period is being treated as a revenue expenditure and will therefore affect your Profit & Loss statement.

If you used to keep manual records of your accounts, the depreciation of your fixed assets was calculated once a year when your auditor presented you with your final accounts. But with the help of computerized records depreciation can be calculated on a monthly basis giving you a more accurate picture of the value of your fixed assets at any given time.

One of two ways is used to calculate depreciation, depending on the type of fixed asset involved.

1. The Straight-line Instalment Method

As the name suggests, this method will deduct a static or equal instalment every month, based on a fixed percentage of the total value of the fixed asset at the start of the financial year. For example, your computer system has cost you £2,000 and has an estimated working life of five years. In each of those five years £400 will be charged to the Profit & Loss account for depreciation, and the asset shown in the Balance Sheet will be reduced by the same amount.

But let us imagine that it is expected that the computer system will be sold for £200 at the end of the five years. The yearly instalment will then be £360, and at the end of the five years the asset will be worth £200, for which it will be sold.

2. The Reducing Instalment Method

With this method the charge for depreciation is based on the percentage of the book value of the asset at the beginning of the financial year.

For example, at the beginning of the year the value of the shop premises, which your business owns, was £10,000, and the depreciation percentage is to be 1% per annum. At the end of the year £100 (1% of £10,000) will be charged to the Profit & Loss account and the value of the asset will be £9,900.

At the end of the second year 1% will be deducted from £9,900, resulting in a £99 instalment, and leaving the value of the asset at the end of the second year at £9,801.

At this rate the value of the asset will not have reached zero at the end of the ten years.

Recording Depreciation

1. Open the Journal window within the Nominal Ledger.

2. Enter the depreciation double entry, using the Depreciation Asset account and the Depreciation Expenses account.

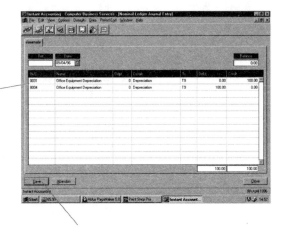

3. Click save to post the double entry before running the Month End procedure.

The Year End Procedure

This option will run all your financial year-end accounting. The Profit & Loss accounts will be transferred to the Retained Earnings account, and the balances of your Balance Sheet will be carried forward to the next year to give an accurate picture of the business's financial state.

Starting Year End

1. Make sure the last month's Month End procedure is completed.

You will be able to enter transactions for the new financial year before running the Year End procedure.

2. Make sure the program date is set at the last day of the last month of your financial year.

Continue with the following procedure:

1 Back up your data files.

2 Move to the Instant Accounting menu bar and click on Defaults.

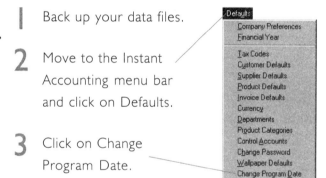

Make sure to change the program date to the last day of your financial year.

3 Click on Change Program Date.

4 Change the date to the last day of the financial year.

5 Click OK.

...contd

6 Move to the Instant Accounting menu bar and click on Period End.

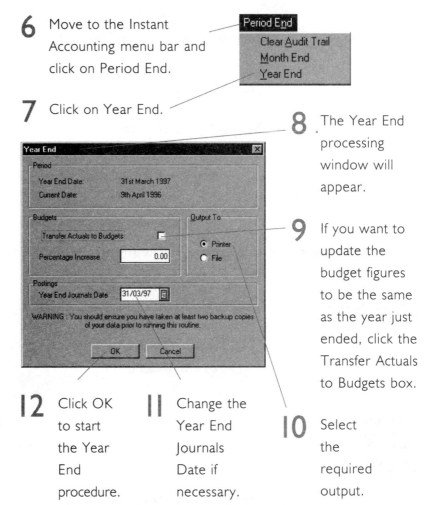

7 Click on Year End.

8 The Year End processing window will appear.

9 If you want to update the budget figures to be the same as the year just ended, click the Transfer Actuals to Budgets box.

HANDY TIP **Use the Calendar button to enter the required Year End Journals Date.**

12 Click OK to start the Year End procedure.

11 Change the Year End Journals Date if necessary.

10 Select the required output.

After the Year End procedure has finished you should run another data file backup. You should keep one copy on-site and one off-site for security reasons.

Before you start to post transactions for the new year you can remove any unwanted Customer, Supplier, Nominal, Bank and Product records. Run Oops! to compress your data files and check that the system start date for the new financial year is correct.

Clearing the Audit Trail

The Clear Audit Trail option can be run when you run your Month End or Year End procedures. Instant Accounting can store up to 2,000,000,000 Audit Trail transactions, and you may never have to clear the Audit Trail until you feel that your system resources are not powerful enough. Whenever Instant Accounting runs reporting procedures it extracts the necessary information from the Audit Trail. Therefore, if the Audit Trail is very large it will slow down your system.

You should also print out the Audit Trail before clearing it, and your data files should be backed up.

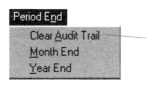

| From the Instant Accounting menu bar click on Period End and then Clear Audit Trail.

Use the Calendar button to enter the required Audit Trail dates.

2 Transactions prior to this entered date will be cleared.

3 Click OK.

The Layout Editor

The Layout Editor lets you easily design new output files or change existing ones.

1 Start the Layout Editor either by using the Windows 95 "Start" program button or by pressing F12.

2 After clicking on the File menu choose the Open option.

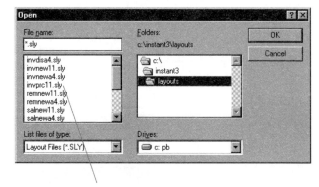

3 Choose the layout file you want to change.

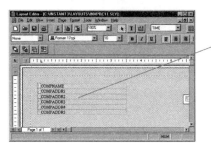

4 Now you can start to make the necessary changes. Don't forget to save the file before you exit the program.

CHAPTER TEN

Opening Balances

This chapter explains how to enter opening balances using the Standard VAT scheme or VAT Cash Accounting scheme.

Covers

Introduction

Whichever VAT scheme you are using when entering the opening balances, Instant Accounting will let you do it quickly and efficiently. The opening balances are very important, because when you first install the Instant Accounting program all accounts in all the ledgers have a zero balance.

It is acceptable to start with zero balances at any time, but if you have been in business for some time then you will already have a transaction history. In previous chapters you may have noticed the option Opening Balance in the Record Detail dialog boxes of the Customer, Supplier and Nominal Ledgers. This is where you must enter the financial position of your business when you start to use Instant Accounting.

Opening balances inform you of the following:

* Outstanding customer transactions

* Outstanding supplier transactions

* Nominal Ledger trial balance

* Stock levels

Without these balances it is impossible for Instant Accounting to show accurate financial statements.

VAT Considerations

Instant Accounting will allow you to account for your VAT in two different ways: Standard VAT and VAT Cash Accounting.

The Standard scheme will calculate VAT transactions whenever invoices within the Customer and Supplier Ledgers are raised, and when bank transactions are performed, including journal entries whenever tax codes other than T9 are used.

On the other hand, VAT Cash Accounting will only calculate VAT when customer receipts and supplier payments are transacted, when bank receipts and payments are made, or when journal entries are performed using tax codes other than T9.

Allocation Considerations

When invoices, credit notes, payments and receipts transactions are entered, they will remain visible until the corresponding debit or credit entry is made. When opening balances are entered as lump sums, it could happen that you can only part-allocate receipts or payments. But if the opening balances are entered as individual transactions then payments and receipts can be allocated accordingly.

Ageing Considerations

If the opening balances are entered as individual transactions then the Aged Balances reports will show a more accurate reading.

When to Enter Opening Balances

After entering the record details of your customers, suppliers, Nominal accounts and Bank accounts then the opening balances should be entered.

Make sure you enter the customer and supplier balances first, before you enter the Nominal accounts' opening trial balances. The customer and supplier balances will have to be cleared before entering the opening trial balance of the Nominal Ledger, because any transaction made in the Supplier and Customer Ledgers will automatically be transacted within the Nominal Ledger.

Opening Balances and Standard VAT Scheme

Opening Balances for Customers and Suppliers

If you are using the Standard VAT scheme, enter your opening balances in the following way:

1 Click on the Customer or Supplier Ledger icon.

2 The Customer or Supplier Records list will appear. Click on the required record.

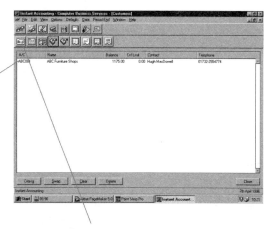

3 Click on the Records icon.

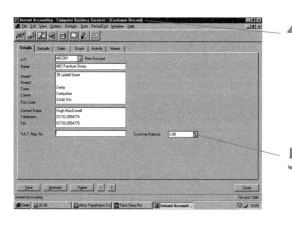

4 The Customer or Supplier Record Details dialog box will appear.

5 Click on the Customer or Supplier Opening Balance button.

...contd

6 The Opening Balance Setup window will appear.

7 Enter a reference.

8 Enter the transaction date.

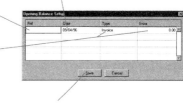

If you are using the original transaction date then the correct aged history will be reported.

9 Select the correct type and enter the amount in the Gross box.

10 Click Save to post.

To Zero the Trial Balance
Make sure to print a trial balance before clearing the balances.

Move into the Nominal Ledger and click on the Journal icon. Using your trial balance output, identify the accounts you wish to zero-balance. For example:

If you enter balances for a number of customers or suppliers, use the < and > buttons to move between them.

Name	Tc	Debit	Credit
Your trial balance:			
Debtors Control account	T9	2000.00	
Creditors Control account	T9		1000.00
Suspense account	T9		1000.00
Your journal entry:			
Debtors Control account	T9		2000.00
Creditors Control account	T9	1000.00	
Suspense account	T9	1000.00	

...contd

Opening Balances for Nominal Ledger or Bank Account

 The balances within the Customer and Supplier Ledgers must be cleared before entering balances in the Nominal Ledger.

1 From the main window click on the Nominal Ledger icon.

2 Click on the required account.

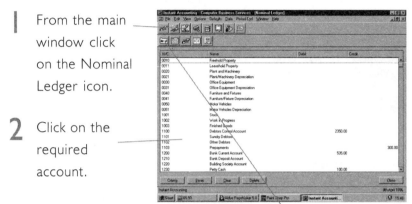

 A liability should always have a credit entry, and an asset should always have a debit entry.

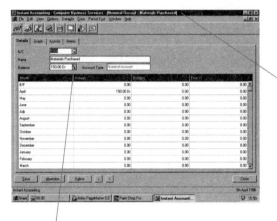

3 Click on the Record icon.

4 The Nominal Account Record Details dialog box will appear.

5 Click on the Opening Balance button.

6 The Opening Balance Setup window will open.

7 Enter the correct balance and then Save.

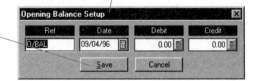

Opening Balances and VAT Cash Accounting

When using the VAT Cash Accounting scheme, VAT rates must be entered with every individual customer or supplier transaction, because VAT is only taken into consideration when payment is being made.

To enter the opening balances for your suppliers and customers use the Batch Invoices screen.

1 From the main window click on the Customer or Supplier icon.

2 Choose the Customer or Supplier record and click to highlight.

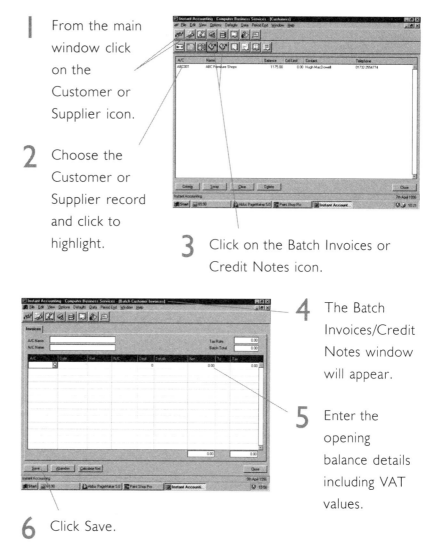

3 Click on the Batch Invoices or Credit Notes icon.

4 The Batch Invoices/Credit Notes window will appear.

5 Enter the opening balance details including VAT values.

6 Click Save.

No Full Opening Trial Balance

It is likely that you will not have been supplied with an opening trial balance from your accountant when you start to use Instant Accounting. There might be some information that you have already, such as the customer and supplier lists, to enter some of the record details. You may also have the bank balance from your bank statement. Such information can be entered and the opening trial balances can be included at a later stage.

Please note that any balances entered before receiving the opening trial balance will also enter a corresponding debit or credit entry into the Suspense account. These balances will need to be adjusted when the entire opening trial balance is supplied.

CHAPTER ELEVEN

Data Management

This chapter explains system management, how to back up data files and how to restore them. It also covers Oops!, which contains various data management tools, and shows how to perform global changes.

Covers

System Management & Security

System management and security are very important for accurate input and output control. As mentioned earlier, incorrect input will result in wrong output, which in turn could interfere with making correct management decisions.

What is system management? Your computer controls and manages many files, which are used by the system or software creating data files, such as your bookkeeping ledgers. Imagine an old filing cabinet with several drawers. If you continuously added files to it, without proper indexing or management, then before too long it would become a complete mess. Therefore proper housekeeping, such as putting files in the correct drawers (i.e., directories), or deleting unwanted files, is necessary. This type of maintenance should be performed on a regular basis.

What do we understand by "security"? Let us say that a fire destroyed your office and all your paper files were lost. Years ago it required mountains of duplicated files being stored in a separate warehouse to secure your business's financial records as required by legislation. Today, using media such as magnetic diskettes or CD-ROMS, you can copy important files and store them easily. It is possible, therefore, to make these vital backups cheaply and regularly. Two copies should be made, one being kept in the office and one in a remote location.

You should refer to your computer software manual and the Windows Backup Help screens for details on security and archiving.

Backing Up

It is very important that you back up your Instant Accounting data files on a regular basis. Although it is rare that major disasters happen, many hours of hard work could be lost if no backup is available.

There are a number of strategies for backup procedures, and the most common one would be the grandfather-father-son backup sequence. Depending on the volume of data input on a daily basis, it is recommended that a backup is performed at least once a day at the end of the session. That latest daily backup is then what we call the son generation of backup files.

 It is advisable that you run a data check before you run a backup.

The next day another backup is made using a new disk. That will make the previous backup become the day minus 1 backup, also known as the father generation backup. On the third day another new disk is used for the latest backup. Therefore, disk backup day minus 2 will become the grandfather generation, day minus 1 the father generation (which the previous day was the son generation), and the most recent backup will be the new son generation.

If your business is a Monday-Friday operation you may want to adopt the following strategy:

	Mon	Tue	Wed	Thu	Fri
Week 1	A	B	A	B	C
Week 2	A	B	A	B	C

Using this strategy, backup A is used on Mondays and Wednesdays, and backup B on Tuesdays and Thursdays. On Friday a weekly backup is done called backup C. This way if an error or corruption occurs you can fall back on the previous day or the previous week.

...contd

Backing Up Data

1 From the Instant
Accounting menu bar
click on Data.

2 Click on Backup.

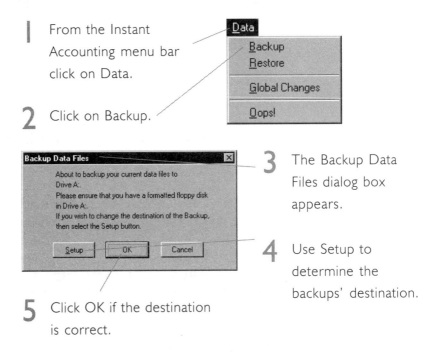

3 The Backup Data
Files dialog box
appears.

4 Use Setup to
determine the
backups' destination.

5 Click OK if the destination
is correct.

 REMEMBER

**Make sure
you label
your
backup
disks with the
correct generation
number and date.**

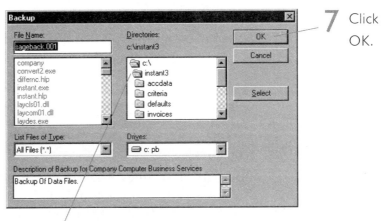

7 Click
OK.

6 Choose the required destination here.

Restore

With any luck you should never have to restore your data files, but if an accident should happen then the Restore procedure will take you back to the backup of your choice. How far back you can go depends on how many generations of backup disks you have.

Restoring Data

 Be sure to run a data check after the completion of the Restore procedure.

1 From the Instant Accounting menu bar click on Data.

2 Click on Restore.

3 The Restore Data Files dialog box will appear.

 You must restore all data files; you cannot restore a part of your data files, such as assets.dta only. Never use the MS-DOS Copy command to restore individual files.

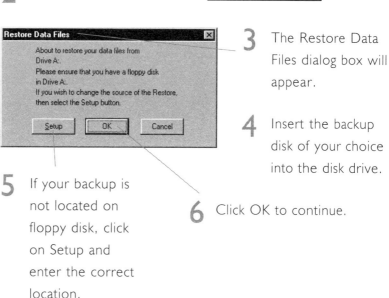

4 Insert the backup disk of your choice into the disk drive.

5 If your backup is not located on floppy disk, click on Setup and enter the correct location.

6 Click OK to continue.

Global Changes

Should you need to change details inside all of your customer or supplier records, such as credit limits, it would be hard work having to change them individually. That is why you can use the Global Changes procedure to make those changes in one go.

1 From the Instant Accounting menu bar click on Data.

2 Click on Global Changes.

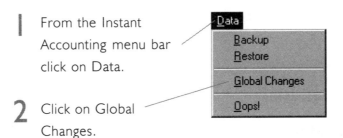

3 The Global Changes Wizard will appear.

4 From the list of options select the area you want to change.

5 Click Next to continue.

6 From the next list of options select the type of change you want to implement.

7 Click Next to continue.

...contd

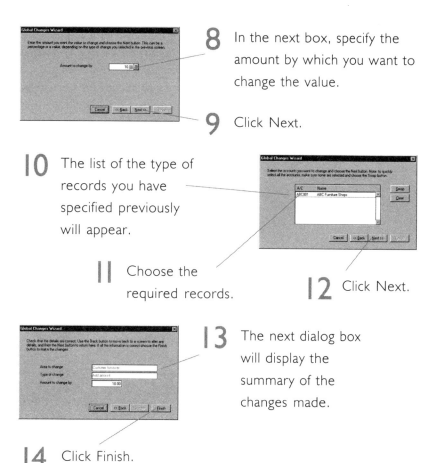

8 In the next box, specify the amount by which you want to change the value.

9 Click Next.

10 The list of the type of records you have specified previously will appear.

 You can Cancel at any stage of the Global Changes procedure.

11 Choose the required records.

12 Click Next.

13 The next dialog box will display the summary of the changes made.

14 Click Finish.

Oops!

Oops! (Disk Doctor) has a number of useful data management tools to check the validity of your data files. After removing a number of records at the start of a new financial year, the data file compression may return some vital disk space.

Oops! will check your data files for the following:

- Input error

- Internal inconsistencies

- Missing data

- Corrupt data

Starting Oops!

1 From the Instant Accounting menu bar click on Data.

2 Click on Oops!

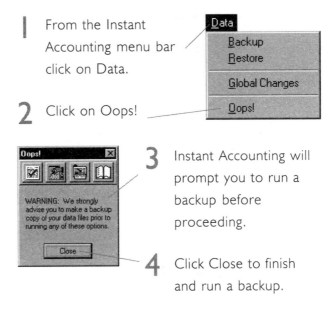

3 Instant Accounting will prompt you to run a backup before proceeding.

4 Click Close to finish and run a backup.

...contd

The Oops! Iconbar

1   Run the Check program.

2   Run the Correct program.

3   Run the Compress program.

4   Run the Rebuild program.

Oops! Check

1   Click this icon to run the Check program.

2 The program will check all ledgers.

Checking Data Files

Checking ledger transaction links

51%

Cancel

3 The program will report any errors.

Oops!

No problems to report on data files.

OK

4 Click OK to finish.

...contd

Oops! Correct

 1   Click this icon to run the Correct program.

2   The Posting Error
    Corrections window
    will appear.

3   Choose the transaction.

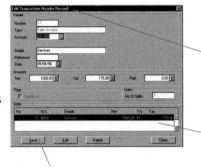

4   Click the Edit button.

5   The Edit Transaction
    Header Record window
    will appear.

REMEMBER

**On VAT
reconciled
transactions
the Reverse
button will show
instead of the
Delete button.**

6   Make the necessary
    changes.

7   Click Save when finished.

On the Transaction Header Record you can amend the
Account (Customer & Supplier), Bank, Details, Reference,
Date and Bank Reconciled Flag.

On the Transaction Split Record you can amend the
Nominal Account, Details, Department, Amount, VAT
Amount and VAT Code.

On the Transaction Allocation Record you can amend the
Reference.

...contd

Oops! Compress

 | Click this icon to run the Compress program.

2 The program will
start to compress
all data files.

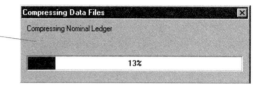

Oops! Rebuild

 | Click this icon to run the Rebuild program.

2 The Rebuild Data Files
window will appear.

3 Select the data file to be
rebuilt by selecting or
deselecting the
appropriate check-boxes.

4 Click OK.

Helpful Tools

The following tools can be helpful when entering transactions.

Whenever you need to enter account codes within the Customer, Supplier or Nominal Ledgers, click the cursor inside the Account Code box and press F4 to bring up the Accounts List.

Press F2 to bring up the calculator.

Use the mouse pointer to enter the values and operate the calculator.

Press F1 to enter the Instant Accounting Help menu.

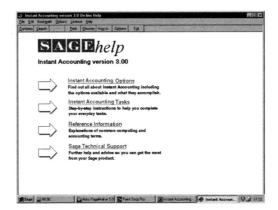

CHAPTER TWELVE

Payroll, Taxes and More

This chapter explains additional taxation liabilities, such as PAYE and National Insurance, and introduces Sage Payroll. Other matters discussed include how to dispose of a fixed asset and how to enter hire purchase agreements.

Covers

The British Taxation System

Every country in the world raises taxes, and there is no reason why Britain should be any different. Why do we have taxes? The answer is, so that the Government can pay for things like the National Health Service, Social Services and national defence.

There are many ways the Government raises taxes, but they can be divided into two parts, direct and indirect tax. The direct tax with which the individual is concerned is more commonly known as income tax, and is evaluated proportionally to the individual's income. It is called direct, because it is charged directly to the individual, and he or she has no choice with regard to paying it.

Indirect tax is collected by many different means. One way known to everybody is Valued Added Tax, or VAT for short. It is a tax added to goods or services sold and charged to the consumer. Other indirect taxes are applied to cigarettes, alcohol and petrol, and are sometimes referred to as duties.

There are many different taxation rules, a full discussion of which would fill volumes, but here we will concern ourselves only with the two main tax liabilities your business will encounter – Pay As You Earn (PAYE) and, as already mentioned, VAT.

Let us start at the top of the hierarchy. The Treasury is the Government's ministry concerned with taxation affairs, and the board is made up of the Prime Minister, the Chancellor of the Exchequer and a number of other senior members known as Lords of the Treasury.

The two bodies responsible for the collection of the above-mentioned taxes are the Department of Inland Revenue and Customs and Excise.

The Inland Revenue is made up of civil servants who are appointed by the Queen. The head office is located in London, with many regional offices under the direction of Her Majesty's Inspector of Taxes.

There are also the Collectors of Taxes, who are appointed by the Inland Revenue to collect taxes as determined by the Inspector of Taxes.

The accounting period in which the Government collects the taxes runs between the 6th April and the 5th April of the following year.

Each year the Chancellor makes changes and improvements to the ruling of the taxation system for the following year, and announces them in his Budget speech in the House of Commons, where it will be discussed and ruled upon. This Finance Bill then becomes the Finance Act, making it an Act of Parliament and hence the country's law.

Every year in March, the Inland Revenue sends instructions for the following fiscal year to all employers, informing them of all necessary changes to the process of tax collection, such as allowances and tax codes. Employers are instructed to collect taxes from their employees on a regular basis and then forward it to the Inland Revenue. There will be more about that in the PAYE section, so let us now move on to Income Tax.

Income Tax & Allowances

There are a number of different ways for one to earn income, and for that reason different income tax rules apply to different sources. Inland Revenue works on six schedules, A, B, C, D, E and F, where business profits are taxed under schedule D and employment income is based on schedule E.

At the time of writing, the percentages used to apply taxation to personal income were 20%, 25% and 40%. By using the Sage Payroll system you will not have to worry about calculating the payment levels, because the program will work that out automatically.

But if you were to collect your gross wages every time, then at the end of the fiscal year you would be confronted with a rather large tax bill from the Inland Revenue. Therefore a system has been established to enable you to make tax payments relative to your salary on a regular basis. For that reason a certain amount is deducted from your gross wages every payday, and the employer is responsible for forwarding the collected tax liabilities of his employees to the Inland Revenue on a monthly basis.

When you have to enter the personal details of your employees into your computer a number of necessary criteria have to be included.

Every person is entitled to a certain allowance, which is a tax-free amount deducted from the gross wages before calculating tax liability. There are a number of different allowances, e.g., for single people, married people or blind people. The program will calculate the correct allowance based on the information given in the Employee Details screen.

PAYE

PAYE stands for Pay As You Earn and, as explained before, it allows you to make tax liability payments on a regular basis, so that you do not face a large tax bill at the end of the year.

At the end of every month the employer collects all the taxes and then forwards them to the Inland Revenue. The tax month runs from the 6th to the 5th of the following month, and payment must be made within fourteen days. Hence, the Inland Revenue PAYE liability payment must be made by the 19th of every month.

Once the payroll has been processed, the payment report, which informs the employer of the breakdown of the different liabilities, should be produced. If the payroll is run on a weekly basis, the tax liability will have to be added up to cover the accounting month. The report will show the total gross and net payroll liability and also the PAYE and National Insurance payments due.

So let us move on and talk about the other liability that employers and employees face with every payroll processed – National Insurance contributions.

National Insurance

National Insurance, a liability to everyone who is earning income, is collected by the Contribution Agency, which manages the National Insurance Fund. The purpose of this fund is to provide benefits, assistance or facilities to the unemployed, elderly and sick.

A number of benefits, such as medical treatment, are available to everybody, but others are only available to people who have made a certain number of contributions.

Everyone earning a certain minimum level of income must pay National Insurance contributions, the amount being determined by the income level and status of the individual. Everyone paying National Insurance is provided with a National Insurance number, which is that person's account number, set by the Contribution Agency.

There are four classes of National Insurance payments. Class 1 is for any employed person, and both the employee and employer will have to make a certain contribution. Your Payroll software will calculate the correct contribution amount as long as the employee details are entered correctly.

Class 2 is a flat-rate contribution paid by people with self-employed status. These people may claim for Sickness Benefit, but not for Unemployment Benefit, since they are not on the market for employment.

Class 3 is a flat-rate voluntary contribution for anyone who wishes to continue payments due to broken employment or other reasons which may cause him or her not to be eligible for certain benefits.

Class 4 is an additional contribution for the self-employed. Class 2 has to be paid regardless of how much a self-employed person earns, but if a certain amount is reached then Class 4 is calculated as a percentage based on the remaining income. Sometimes it is impossible to determine the entire income if you are self-employed, so Class 4 liability is calculated at the end of the financial year when income is declared to the Inland Revenue.

Statutory Sick Pay

An employee covered by the National Insurance scheme is eligible for Sickness Benefit. It is initially paid by the employer, who can claim it back according to a certain percentage and variations – unless the business did not exceed a set yearly amount, in which case the lot can be reclaimed from the Contribution Agency.

The Sage Payroll software will make the sickness payments automatically, provided the correct dates and employee details have been entered.

Statutory Maternity Pay

As with Statutory Sick Pay, Maternity Pay is also provided by the employer, and can be claimed back. Payments are 90% of earnings for a period of six weeks, plus a fixed amount.

The employee is only eligible for SMP if she has been employed for the last 26 weeks continuously, with average weekly earnings equal to the lower earnings limits for NI contributions.

Again, the Sage Payroll software will calculate the correct SMP payments, provided the correct dates and employee details have been entered.

P45

When an employee changes his or her employment, the new employer must be informed of the person's accumulated gross pay and contributions made to PAYE and NI so far, in order to be able to make the correct deductions.

Therefore, when an employee leaves his or her post the employer will provide a P45, which is a form providing the necessary information. This form has three copies, one of which is retained by the past employer, one by the employee and one which is handed over to the future employer.

The Sage Payroll software has a P45 option which will print out the necessary information automatically once the employee is made a "Leaver".

Payroll Year-End

After your last payroll of the financial year is completed, the Sage Payroll system makes the end-of-year procedure very simple. You will never want to go back to a manual process.

There are two forms provided by the Inland Revenue at the end of the financial year, the P14 and the P35.

The P14 is the income and contribution details form, which will have to be completed for every employee, and the P35 is a summary sheet of the same amounts.

Both forms can be printed out by the computer system, and the end-of-year procedure, which used to take hours, can now be completed in minutes.

The P14 is in three parts, one being retained by the employer and the other two being forwarded to the Contribution Agency and the Inland Revenue. The P35 is also sent to the Inland Revenue.

After the backups have been completed, the update program, provided by Sage, can be run, preparing your system for the next financial year. Any changes made in the previous Budget will be included in the update disk, and any possible worries you might have concerning correct liability calculations for the next year are dispelled.

Disposal of a Fixed Asset

Fixed assets are not normally intended for resale, but on occasion you may have reason to sell or exchange them.

If the asset is sold for more than its net value then it is known as a gain and becomes a part of your revenue income. On the other hand, if the asset is sold for less than the net value then you have a loss.

In both cases the transactions are to be made as a journal entry. You may want to ask your accountant for assistance so that you can be assured that the disposal has been accounted for correctly.

First, the correct depreciation value at the time of sale has to be calculated, and then the balance of the fixed asset will be reduced by that amount. Depending on the selling price, the balance of the fixed asset may be in debit or credit once the double entry has been made between the Bank account and the Asset account. Whatever is left over will have to be transacted between the Asset account and the Profit & Loss account, hence calculating the revenue profit or loss.

Hire Purchase Agreement

Sometimes you may want to purchase an asset on hire purchase, meaning that ownership does not belong to you or your business until it has been paid off.

Motor vehicles are often purchased on hire, the benefit of this being that it allows someone to purchase an asset over a period of time, without needing to have the funds to pay for it at the outset.

The hire purchase company will charge interest on the loan, and the signed agreement will show the capital borrowed and the interest charged. The total will be more than the value of the car when initially purchased.

Motor Vehicle	10,000
HP interest 10%	1,000
Total cost of car	11,000

Let us say, for example, that you paid a £2,000 deposit and that the monthly repayments are £150.

The first journal entry would be the value of the car, debiting the Motor Vehicle account by £10,000 and crediting the Hire Purchase Company (Liability) account also by £10,000. This takes care of the vehicle purchase value, or its capital cost.

Next, the £2,000 deposit will have to be transacted. This is done by crediting the Bank account and debiting the Hire Purchase Company account by £2,000, hence reducing your capital liability down to £8,000.

Whenever you make a monthly instalment you have to work out how much of it is capital expenditure and how much is the interest, which is revenue expenditure. The cost of the interest is incurred by the purchase of the asset and is therefore a revenue expense and not a capital expense. It is best to contact the hire purchase company for a breakdown of the monthly payments between capital and interest, because the APR, on which interest is calculated, can be a little tricky to work out.

So, on a monthly basis you can credit the Bank account by £150, debit the capital amount (i.e., £100) from the Hire Purchase Company account and debit the HP Interest account (Expense account) by the interest amount (i.e., £50). At the bottom the debit and credit columns should balance at £150, and you can save the transaction.

At the end of the agreement the Motor Vehicle account will have depreciated in accordance with the depreciation amount recorded in the Profit & Loss account. The Hire Purchase Company account will have a zero balance and the HP Interest account will have a total debit balance of £1,000.

Index

A

Account payee only   63
Accounting
  Equation   24
  Period   100
  Principles   8
  Software   9
Accruals   43
Activity Window   41
Aged balances   52
Assets   32
Audit   8
  Fees   8
  Trail   97-98

B

Backing up   131
Balance Sheet   26-28
Bank   62-78
  Account Details   65
  Iconbar   64
  Payment   66
  Receipt   71
  Reconciliation   75-76
  Reports   78
  Statements   75-77
Batch invoices   50
Bookkeeping   8, 32-34
Budget value   39
Building Society account   62
Business transactions   17, 21

C

Calculator   140
Cash account   69
Chancellor of the Exchequer   142
Chart of Accounts   38, 44-46
  Dialog Box   45
Clear Audit Trail   119
Clearing   63
Collectors of Taxes   143
Communication software   10
Company details   13
Company Setup   13
Computer manuals   10
Contribution Agency   146
Control accounts   39
  Defaults   16
Corrupt data   136
Cost of Sale   22
Credit   32, 52, 59
Credit Card account   62, 67
Credit notes   49, 53, 60, 86
Credit purchase   84
Current account   62
Current Assets   36
Customer
  Accounts   42, 51
  Activity window   51
  Defaults   15
  Desktop   49
  Iconbar   48
  Ledger   48-54
  Letters   49
  Receipt   72
  Records   49
Customs & Excise   21, 108